PUB WALKS
The Dorset Co

TWENTY CIRCULAR WALKS

Anne-Marie Edwards

COUNTRYSIDE BOOKS
NEWBURY, BERKSHIRE

First published 1997
© Anne-Marie Edwards

Revised and updated 1999, 2002, 2005

COUNTRYSIDE BOOKS
3 Catherine Road
Newbury, Berkshire

To view our complete range of books,
please visit us at
www.countrysidebooks.co.uk

ISBN 1 85306 464 5

*For my very good friends Nick and Suzanne,
with love and thanks.*

Designed by Graham Whiteman
Cover illustration by Colin Doggett
Photographs by Mike Edwards
Maps by Trevor Yorke

Produced through MRM Associates Ltd., Reading
Printed by J.W. Arrowsmith Ltd., Bristol

Contents

Walk

PUBLISHER'S NOTE

We hope that you obtain considerable enjoyment from this book; great care has been taken in its preparation. However, changes of landlord and actual closures are sadly not uncommon. Likewise, although at the time of publication all routes followed public rights of way or permitted paths, diversion orders can be made and permissions withdrawn.

We cannot of course be held responsible for such diversion orders and any inaccuracies in the text which result from these or any other changes to the routes nor any damage which might result from walkers trespassing on private property. We are anxious though that all details covering the walks and the pubs are kept up to date and would therefore welcome information from readers which would be relevant to future editions.

Acknowledgements
It is a pleasure to acknowledge the help I have received from the many people I have met while walking the Dorset Coast Path. Grateful thanks to the staff of the Dorset Tourist Information Offices especially in Lyme Regis, to George Elliott, Head Warden of the Golden Cap Estate, Rupert Van Haght and Mr and Mrs Wraxall for information on Seatown and Mrs Joan Brachi for fascinating details about Kimmeridge. For help and encouragement I would like to thank Dorset author Harry Ashley and Capt Roger Frampton. The National Trust information centres have been invaluable. I would also like to acknowledge the excellent account of National Trust properties given in Rodney Legg's *Dorset National Trust Guide*. For help in revising the route of the Coast Path for this edition, I am most grateful to Adrian Brokenshire, the Dorset Countryside Ranger, and Mr P. Press at Charmouth Parish Council. As always, the staff of Southampton and Totton libraries have provided me with help and friendly advice as well as books. Finally I thank my good friends Mary and Ken Chambers for their cheerful support and my husband Mike who takes the photographs and without whom this book would never have been written.

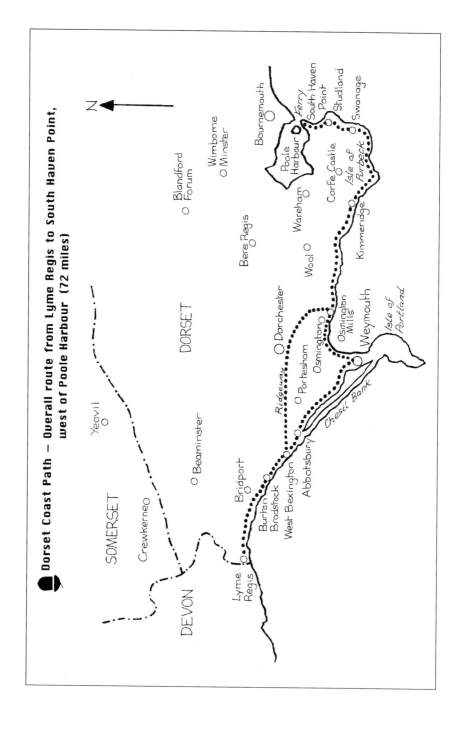

Dorset Coast Path – Overall route from Lyme Regis to South Haven Point, west of Poole Harbour (72 miles)

N

SOMERSET

DEVON

DORSET

Crewkerne○

Yeovil○

○Beaminster

Lyme Regis○

Bridport○

Burton Bradstock○

West Bexington

Abbotsbury

Chesil Bank

Ridgeway ○Dorchester

○Portesham

Osmington○

Osmington Mills○

Weymouth

Isle of Portland

Bere Regis○

Wool○

Wareham○

Kimmeridge○

Isle of Purbeck

Corfe Castle○

Poole Harbour

Bournemouth○

Ferry

South Haven Point

Studland○

Swanage○

○Blandford Forum

Wimborne ○Minster

INTRODUCTION

● The magnificent scenery of the Dorset Coast Path is justly famous.
It is the shortest of the four sections of the 594 mile long South
West Coast Path, running east for 72 miles from Lyme Regis Bay to
South Haven Point on the west shore of Poole Harbour. Throughout its
length it commands a breathtaking coastline. The wide sweep of Lyme
Regis Bay is fringed by many-coloured cliffs composed of alternate
layers of greensand, limestone and clay which rise to the highest point
on the south coast at Golden Cap. The sheer walls of sandstone at West
Bay, Bridport's tiny harbour, are protected by the western end of one of
the Dorset coast's unique features, the Chesil Bank. This great pebble
ridge has resisted the force of the waves since prehistoric times and
runs for over 18 miles to Portland Bill. Trapped behind lie the quiet
waters of the Fleet, 8 miles in length and England's most extensive
lagoon. By contrast, the Isle of Purbeck defies the sea with massive
slabs of limestone dark with the caverns of former quarries, and
spectacular cliffs of dazzlingly white chalk. Combined with this natural
beauty is a rich store of fascinating history and a wealth of wildlife. So it
comes as no surprise that, under Enterprise Neptune, the National Trust
now owns a third of the land crossed by the Coast Path.

But there is another Dorset waiting to be discovered by the walker. It
is a world of small villages tucked away from the sea in the hollows of
the downs, reached by lanes and footpaths through woods full of
wildflowers and birdsong. Old manors built of local stone stand beside
simple churches often dating from before the Norman Conquest. Dark-
thatched cottages line quiet streets where time seems to have stood
still. This book offers an opportunity to explore both worlds.

All the 20 circular pub walks include a section of the Coast Path and
part of the nearby countryside, revealing different facets of the often
hidden beauty of Dorset. These walks are all safe and moderate in
length, varying from 2½ to 5½ miles. They are suitable for all the
family. If you wish to walk the Coast Path as a linear route, special links
are provided between each chapter. The section of Coast Path which
the walk follows is indicated by the acorn logo, the symbol used to
mark long-distance footpaths. Generally the Coast Path is well signed
with acorn logos on footpaths and stiles. Sometimes elegant round-
topped markers of Purbeck stone are set along the route. The Coast
Path is not marked through Swanage and Weymouth so I have
included detailed directions. Between West Bexington and Osmington

Mills the Coast Path offers a choice between a northern route following the South Dorset Ridgeway, which avoids Weymouth and reduces the distance by 6 miles, and a southern route which runs beside the Fleet. For the purposes of the pub walks I have chosen the northern route for its spectacular views, variety of scenery and historic interest. But I also include a section (at the end of chapter 6) giving directions for linear Coast Path walkers wishing to follow the southern route.

The walks start and finish at a good pub chosen for its home-cooking and interesting character. In Dorset it is still possible to come across real village pubs with flagged floors, heavily beamed ceilings and locally brewed ales of excellent quality. You will find some of these establishments in this book but in all the pubs you can be sure of a friendly welcome. Many of the village pubs are small so at holiday times it is advisable to book your meal in advance. Telephone numbers are given, as well as details of parking and opening times.

A note on the Coast Path itself: Although it reaches no great height at any point, some climbing is usually involved. In these cases allow plenty of time to rest and enjoy the view! Wear shoes or boots with a good grip as the going can become slippery after rain. Take extra care wherever the Path runs close to the edge of overhanging cliffs. I have mentioned these places in the text to give clear warning. There is always the danger that these unstable cliffs may slip at any time so do follow any diversion signs that may be in force. The wildlife is spectacular so it is quite a good idea to carry binoculars.

The sketch maps in this book are designed only as simple guides to the starting points of the walks and are intended to provide an overall view of the routes. For more detailed information I recommend you arm yourself with the relevant Ordnance Survey Landranger map noted in the introduction to each walk. As the Path runs through a popular holiday area it is usually possible to find accommodation and campsites either on the route or within a reasonable distance. A note on accommodation and a list of useful addresses will be found at the end of the book.

Finally I wish you many happy hours walking this splendid Coast Path and exploring the beautiful Dorset countryside through which it passes.

Anne-Marie Edwards

LYME REGIS
The Cobb Arms

Magnificent clifftop views, hidden valleys and flower-filled meadows are features of this walk. You can visit the historic town of Lyme Regis before exploring the lovely countryside to the north of the town and returning by a riverside path.

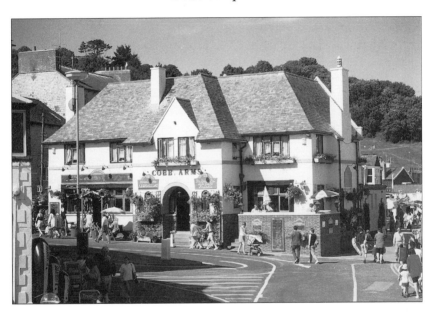

A little to the west of Lyme Regis a cluster of houses overlook the town's famous Cobb, a massive stone breakwater curved like a protecting arm shielding the fishing boats and pleasure craft in the harbour from the force of seas whipped up by south-westerly gales. At the foot of the cliffs, facing this tiny harbour, is the Cobb Arms, a large, friendly, welcoming pub with plenty of room for families. As the pub also offers accommodation it makes an ideal starting point for the Dorset Coast Path.

Hot food is served from 10 am to 10 pm – ideal hours for the walker – and sandwiches and light refreshments are also available. There is a very wide range of good food on offer, including whole dressed crab. Popular with locals and visitors alike are French sticks crammed with a variety of delicious fillings. Drinking hours are from 10 am to 11 pm, 12 noon to 10.30 pm on Sundays. The Cobb Arms is a Palmers house and among the real ales on offer is their Bicentenary Ale. Others include Bridport Bitter and IPA. Taunton Traditional cider makes a pleasant alternative. Telephone: 01297 443242.

- **HOW TO GET THERE:** To avoid driving through Lyme Regis, which can become congested with traffic, turn off the A35 along the B3165, signed 'Uplyme'. Drive through Uplyme then turn right along the A3052 (Exeter road), signed for the Cobb. Turn left at the T-junction then almost immediately right down Cobb Road to the harbour. The Cobb Arms is on the left.
- **PARKING:** The pub has no car park but there are large public car parks close by. If these are full, drive back up Cobb Road to a large car park on the left.
- **LENGTH OF THE WALK:** 3½ miles. Map: OS Landranger 193 Taunton and Lyme Regis (inn GR 338917).

THE WALK

From the Cobb Arms it is only a step to the Cobb itself and no-one could possibly resist the temptation to begin this walk with a stroll along one of its two levels, dating from the 14th century. The very steep flight of solid stone steps descending to the Lower Cobb are the famous 'Granny's Teeth' immortalised by Jane Austen in her novel *Persuasion*.

Return to the pub to join the Coast Path.

Leave the front of the pub on your right and turn right down Marine Parade. Opposite Jane's café a small flight of steps leads up to a small garden (look for the bust of Jane Austen on the wall). This is on the site of 'Wings', the boarding house where Jane possibly stayed in 1804. Follow the Parade as it curves round the bay with a splendid view of the colourful houses of Lyme Regis and the foot of the High Street firmly buttressed against the force of the waves. Beyond the town stretches an undulating line of green and gold cliffs striped with bands of dark fossil-rich clay known as blue lias. Cross the High Street and bear right along Broad Street to cross the river Lim, called at this point 'the Buddle'. Continue up the road past the church for a little over a ¼ mile to a stile set diagonally in the hedge beside a footpath sign. Cross the stile and walk diagonally up the meadow. At the top bear right to a stile (ignore the fence on the left). Cross and walk up to the gate you

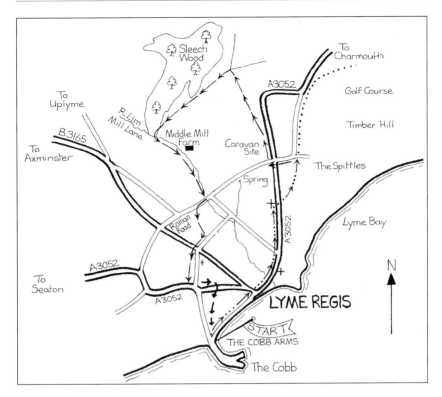

will see ahead by a signpost. Walk up the next field in the direction indicated by the signpost to go through a small gate opening onto a track at The Spittles, an attractive landslip area. Turn left along the track towards a gate. Just before the gate the Coast Path turns right uphill through a wood.

Leave the Coast Path at this point and walk on through the gate to a minor road. Walk down the road to meet the main road, the A3052. Turn right beside the road for about 50 yards then turn left to follow the track – it is a public right of way – running past Timber Hill Caravan Park. Follow the track past the caravans into a valley folded between wooded hillsides. Pass a footpath on the left and keep ahead to a crossing bridleway. Turn left through a small wooden gate, and continue ahead over the meadows beside the ancient oaks and sycamores of Sleech Wood. Follow the blue bridleway signs through several gates, past the waterworks to follow a narrow path running through the wood, carpeted with bluebells in May and June. A little bridge leads you over a stream in front of a thatched cottage. Turn left

11

by the stream to continue through a wooden gate and over a small meadow to a footbridge over the river Lim.

With the river on your left walk down the valley. Footbridges lead you to the other side of the river and the footpath becomes a lane leading to a minor road. Turn right over medieval Horn Bridge and walk a few yards up Roman Road. Turn left past the Woodland Trust sign and follow the field path ahead which shortly divides. Take the right-hand path to the corner of the field, leaving a house on your left. Walk up the next field to a gate opening onto a minor road. Bear right to the main road, the B3165. Cross the main road and follow the road almost directly ahead, Pound Road, past the church on your left to meet the A3052. Turn left over the top of the Cobb road and continue to the entrance to the Gardens on your right. Go through the gate into the Gardens and follow the path down the hillside to Marine Parade. Turn right to return to the Cobb Arms. *Owing to a landslip the Gardens are closed for restoration until summer 2006. Until then return to the Cobb and your car down the Cobb road.*

 LYME REGIS (HARBOUR) TO CHARMOUTH BEACH (2¹⁄₂ MILES)

Follow the route of Walk 1 as far as the track at The Spittles. Turn left towards a gate. Just before the gate leading to a road, leave the route of the walk and turn right uphill through the wood. Follow the steepest path to a signpost at the top of the wood. Bear left following the sign for Charmouth along the top of the hillside. The path runs through the trees then descends steps and drops downhill to meet a minor road. Turn right beside the road for about ¹⁄₄ mile to meet the A3052. Continue ahead along the pavement beside the A3052 for about 100 yards to a footpath sign on the right. Turn right as the sign directs. Our way now leads over the golf course and no clear path is visible but the route is indicated by white stones. Keep ahead leaving low embankments and white stones close on your right to cross the golf course, go over a white path and enter a wood.

Follow the path through the wood to meet the A3052 again. Turn right and follow the pavement beside the road passing a roundabout on your left and walk down into Charmouth village. Turn right along Bridge Road. When the road curves right, keep straight on down the footpath ahead, passsing a phone box on the right. The footpath leads to a narrow lane. Follow this to Lower Sea Lane and turn left to the beach beside the little river Char which, having carved a steep-sided valley through the coastal hills, now loses itself among the pebbles.

CHARMOUTH
The George

*Choose a clear day for this walk as the views throughout are magnificent.
We follow a high seaward-facing ridge, Stonebarrow Hill for about 1¹/₂
miles then descend the hill past St Wite's Well to follow the Coast Path along
the cliff top. An easy climb back to the car park completes a superb walk.*

With the discovery of the benefits of sea bathing in the 18th century,
Charmouth became a fashionable resort and its hillside street is lined
with a wonderfully varied mix of Regency bow-windowed houses and
older thatched cottages. One of the oldest houses of all must be the
George. It is a genuine old-world Dorset inn with stone-flagged floors,
deep window seats, low beams and a splendid inglenook fireplace. It
was built as a farmhouse in 1205 and some windows at what was once
the stable end of the building retain their iron bars. In the 17th century
it became an important coaching inn on the turnpike road between
Exeter and Dorchester. Strong horses were kept in the stables to be

hitched to the coaches to help them up the hilly street. A boy was sent with them to bring the horses safely down again!

Good, satisfying food to suit all tastes is served in the bar area and in the cosy dining room from noon to 2 pm and from 7 pm to 9 pm. The wide range of home-cooked food includes substantial steaks and pies and as a lighter alternative a variety of sandwiches and filled jacket potatoes. There is a special menu for children. Drinking hours in winter are from 11.30 am to 2.30 pm and from 6 pm to 11 pm but in summer the hours are longer. Real ales include Directors, Ruddles Best, John Smith's and George's Bitter. There is a large garden and a covered play area for children. I am told that dogs with well-behaved owners are welcome! The inn offers bed and breakfast. Telephone: 01297 560280.

● **HOW TO GET THERE:** This walk begins from the parking area on the top of Stonebarrow Hill. Approaching from the east, turn for Charmouth off the A35. Continue for a little over 1/4 mile. Just before the road curves right to cross the river Char turn sharp left up Stonebarrow Hill. Cross the cattle grid at the top of the hill and park on the right facing the sea about thirty yards further on. Approaching from the west via Charmouth drive through the village and when the road curves left keep straight on up Stonebarrow Lane and park as above.

● **PARKING:** On the top of Stonebarrow Hill (GR 381933).

● **LENGTH OF THE WALK:** 5 miles. Map: OS Landranger 193 Taunton and Lyme Regis (inn GR 367937).

THE WALK

From the parking area on the top of Stonebarrow Hill bear left along the crest of the ridge – the sea is on your right. Soon you have a breathtaking view eastwards towards Golden Cap. The whole of this walk is in the beautiful Golden Cap estate owned by the National Trust and rich in plants and wildlife. In May, Stonebarrow is thickly carpeted with bluebells. Later yellow bird's foot trefoil, white ox-eye daisies and purple orchids attract a host of butterflies including the Painted Lady and the Brown Argus. Roe deer roam the woods and buzzards soar overhead.

Pass the National Trust Information Centre on your left. (The Centre is open in good weather Easter and May to September.) After about 1½ miles you come to a signpost indicating several paths. Take the path straight ahead signed for Chardown Hill and Morcombelake. Go through a gate and follow the crest of the ridge through another gate. Keep ahead and now you will enjoy a splendid view inland. Beyond the

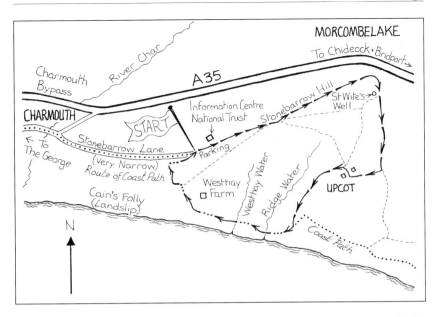

thickly hedged meadows of the Marshwood Vale, rise a range of hills dominated by the county's highest summit, Pilsdon Pen. The path descends through another gate to a lane. Follow the lane downhill to a signpost on the right for St Wite's Well and Golden Cap. Turn right down the track and go through a gate to the open grassy slopes of Chardown Hill. On your right you shortly pass the holy well of St Wite. Here a small stream emerges from the hillside and falls into a stone basin. Thomas Gerard writing in the 1620s describes the little Saxon woman, St Wite, as living 'in prayer and contemplation' near Whitchurch 'not far off in the side of a hill'. Local people have always believed this hillside was her home. Tradition holds that she was killed by the Danes. A small casket containing her remains was recently discovered in the church at Whitchurch Canonicorum but her shrine in the church had been a place of pilgrimage throughout medieval times.

Follow the path downhill to a crosstrack and turn right signed for Stonebarrow and Charmouth along a track leading to Upcot Farm. Walk through the farmyard to a signpost. (At this point the right of way differs slightly from the OS map.) Turn right signed for Stonebarrow and follow the track uphill for about 200 yards to a footpath sign and stile on your left. Turn left over the stile (ignore the other signs) and walk up the grassy ridge ahead to follow the crest past a footpath marker post on your right. Now you are heading west with a

View from Swyre Head, near Kimmeridge.

marvellous view over a line of cliffs descending to Lyme Regis harbour. Keep straight ahead to the far corner of the field slowly descending the ridge to meet a clearer path. Follow the path keeping a hedge on your left. Cross a stile and follow the path along a wide grassy ridge. Keep ahead at the next footpath sign and cross the stile to meet the Coast Path.

Turn right to follow the Coast Path in a westerly direction. Walk down the meadow with a hedge on your right to cross a small wooden footbridge over Ridge Water. Climb the steps on the other side and bear half-right uphill towards some conspicuous wooden fences. Cross the stile between the fences and walk downhill to cross another wooden footbridge over Westhay Water. Keep straight ahead uphill, hedge on your right, towards a post and continue up a meadow with Westhay Farm beyond a small pinewood on your right. Climb the field ahead keeping straight on past a footpath sign with a hedge about 50 yards away on your left. Beyond the low cliff edge rises the new exposed orange sandstone face of Cain's Folly. Cross the stile at the top of the field and walk up steps to a green path by a footpath sign. Turn left and follow the path as it curves right up steps. The steps give way to a track which continues uphill and becomes a grassy path leading to another footpath sign. Bear left again and keep to the path as it curves right with a fence on the left and leads to a prominent footpath sign for the National Trust Information Centre and Stonebarrow. Turn right to walk along a wide path which takes you past a barrier to the parking area on Stonebarrow Hill and your car.

Drive back down Stonebarrow Lane to Charmouth to visit the George inn.

 Charmouth beach to Golden Cap (3½ miles)

From Charmouth beach retrace your steps to the village. At the top of Bridge Road turn right and when the road curves left keep straight on up Stonebarrow Hill to the parking area just past the cattle grid. Turn right here over the grass following the sign for the Coast Path East. Bear a little right past a wooden barrier and follow the path straight ahead over the grass, fence on left. (Ignore a path sharp right leading to a gate, and two other paths on your left.) This leads to a signpost where the path swings left. The path runs beside a fence then curves a little left once more to another signpost. Turn right as directed to continue downhill to descend some steps. Turn left for a few yards then right as the next signpost directs. Cross a stile and follow the Coast Path signs down the meadow with the hedge close on the right. The path is now easy to follow as it crosses more fields not far from the cliff edge, crossing wooden footbridges over Westhay Water and Ridge Water. A steeper ascent leads over Broom Cliff. Ahead rises the distinct profile of the appropriately named Golden Cap with its crown of orange sandstone. A footpath on the left leads to a ruined church and scattering of thatched cottages, all that remains of the village of Stanton St Gabriel. The village declined when coastal erosion destroyed the main road which once ran through it. Climb to the top of Golden Cap and cross the summit past the memorial to the Earl of Antrim to the trig point.

SEATOWN

The Anchor Inn

A delightful walk taking you with very little effort to the top of Golden Cap, the highest cliff on England's south coast. But before arriving at this splendid viewpoint, there is an opportunity to enjoy other aspects of the Dorset countryside – its old coaching roads, now deep sunken lanes bordered by ferns, and wooded hillsides, the haunt of roe deer. The charming village of Chideock is within easy reach.

Seatown is a small fishing hamlet in a secluded bay where the little river Winniford joins the sea. It is sheltered to the west by Golden Cap, an impressive cliff which rises to a height of 618 ft, and to the east by Thorncombe Beacon. The Anchor Inn, situated on a low cliff overlooking the beach, makes the most of this magnificent setting with superb sea views. The huge pebble-encrusted anchor in the pub garden was 'caught' by a local fisherman. It belonged to the *Hope* of Amsterdam wrecked off Chesil Beach in 1748.

The inn serves excellent home-cooked food from 12 noon to 9.30 pm, Whitsun to early September, from 12 noon to 2 pm and 6.30 pm to 9.30 pm the rest of the year. The regular menu contains such delights as home-baked steak and kidney pie, Hot 'n' Spicy Chicken (butterfly chicken breast coated in spices) and 'Memsahib's Curry and Rice', an authentic Indian beef curry, cooked to an old family recipe. There is also a daily specials board and a wide range of sweets. The inn prides itself on serving proper puddings which include apple and marzipan pie and chocolate truffle torte. Children have their own menu and there is a family room.

Drinking hours are 11 am to 11 pm from Whitsun to September, 11 am to 2.30 pm and 6 pm to 10 pm the rest of the year. The Anchor is a Palmers House serving their IPA and Bicentenary Ale and also Tally Ho! and Bridport Bitter. There is a well-chosen wine list. Dogs on leads are welcome. Telephone: 01297 489215.

- **HOW TO GET THERE:** Turn off the A35 opposite the church in Chideock village, following the sign for Seatown. The lane runs for about 3/4 mile to the beach in front of the Anchor Inn.
- **PARKING:** The Anchor has a small car park but at busy times it would be advisable to leave your car in the large public car park opposite.
- **LENGTH OF THE WALK:** 3½ miles plus an optional extension of 3/4 mile around Langdon Wood. Map: OS Landranger 193 Taunton and Lyme Regis (inn GR 420917).

THE WALK

Leave the front of the Anchor Inn on your left and walk up the lane away from the beach. Turn right opposite the shop and information centre down Mill Lane, marked by a 'no access for motors' sign. After a few yards you will see a beautifully restored packhorse bridge over the river Winniford across the field on your right. Pass the mill and Mill Cottage and continue along the lane to a stile on the left and a footpath sign for Seahill and Langdon Hill. Turn left over the stile and walk up the meadow ahead, with the hedge close on the left, towards the woods. Cross the next stile and keep on up the field. At the top of the field turn left by the footpath sign and continue with the hedge on your right to a stile. Turn right over the stile to meet Sea Hill Lane. Bear right up the lane for about 50 yards then leave the road and turn left up a peaceful track, Combrey Lane.

Combrey Lane meets Pettycrate Lane which runs down to Chideock.

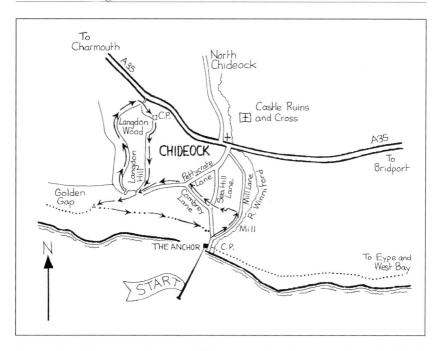

Bear left a little to continue uphill past another lane on the right. Walk past a gate to follow a terraced path beside Langdon Wood to a footpath sign. A path is signed straight ahead over the meadow to Golden Cap but I would recommend that, before you follow it, you should make a circuit of Langdon Wood, about 3/4 mile round, to enjoy fine views of the inland hills. To see Langdon Wood bear right past the barrier, following the sign for the wood, and continue on the path uphill through the beech woods. The gravel gives way to grass and you turn left along a grassy path signed for the Langdon Wood walk. Beech trees shade the path on the right and on the left runs a thick, overgrown coppice hedge, a haven for wildlife. When the path curves a little uphill to meet a crosstrack, bear left to walk round the northern edge of the wood. The path widens as it turns south through mature oaks and beeches to a National Trust car park. Continue straight across and follow the path ahead through the gate to continue to the southern fringe of the wood. The track curves slightly west and divides. Take the gravel track on the left downhill which after a few yards takes you back to the signpost at the beginning of the circuit. Bear left to retrace your steps to the barrier and turn right to follow the path signed for the Coast Path and Golden Cap.

The Dorset cliffs near Seatown.

Follow the path over the fields then climb the stepped path to the trig point on the top of Golden Cap.

 Coast Path walkers join the walk at this point. From the trig point retrace the route down the steps. Go through the gate at their foot and turn right, signed for the Coast Path and Seatown. The path dips over the field to a stile. Cross, go down the steps and follow the path as it descends steeply down the next field. Follow the path along the grassy hillside and across a small valley to a signpost. Climb the stile and follow the woodland path over a small wooden bridge and another stile. A clear path leads over a field. Cross the stile at the other end of the field and follow the path ahead to meet the lane to Seatown. Turn right to walk down to the beach by the Anchor Inn.

GOLDEN CAP TO THORNCOMBE BEACON (2¹/₂ MILES)

Follow Walk 3 from Golden Cap as far as the beach at Seatown. With the Anchor Inn on your left cross the bridge on your right and walk over the car park to a National Trust sign beside a gate and stile. Cross the stile and climb up Ridge Hill. The path dips to a gate and stile at the foot of a steep climb up Doghouse Hill. Keep straight on to the top and you will see Thorncombe Beacon ahead, crowning Thorncombe cliff. When the path divides take the right-hand path (the left-hand one follows a slightly easier gradient but is a less direct route) and walk up to the beacon.

EYPE

The New Inn

A magnificent short ramble including a ridge walk along Eype Down, famous for its panoramic views. The coast is reached at Thorncombe Beacon, which at 508 ft is second only in height to Golden Cap. This less-frequented countryside is particularly rich in wildlife.

Only minutes from the busy A35, Eype is a village straight from the pages of a Thomas Hardy novel. Stone-built thatched cottages perch either side of a narrow lane which descends a steep ravine to the sea. The little school, still with its bell above the porch, is dated 1859. Opposite the school stands the New Inn, a freehouse, offering a warm welcome. Before becoming an inn, it was known as Paradise Cottage and the collections of colourful plates and water jugs decorating the bar area contribute to the pub's particularly attractive atmosphere. An outstanding feature is the terraced garden on a west-facing hillside –

the perfect place to enjoy a relaxing drink in the evening!

A wide range of delicious home-cooked food includes steak and Guinness pie cooked to a special Irish recipe, chunky beef chilli, breaded chicken goujons and several vegetarian dishes. The children's menu is particularly tempting. What child could resist a Sweet Shop Sundae with chocolate buttons or a Candy Shop Surprise? Four real ales are on offer, Palmers Bridport Bitter, IPA, 200 and Tally Ho! Guinness, lager and cider are also available. Dogs on leads are welcome.

Opening times are Monday to Friday from 12 noon to 2.30 pm and 5.30 pm to 11 pm, Saturday from 12 noon to 11 pm and Sunday from 12 noon to 2.30 pm and 7 pm to 10.30 pm. Meals are served on Monday to Saturday from 12 noon to 2 pm and 6 pm to 10 pm and on Sunday from 12 noon to 2 pm and 7 pm to 9.30 pm. Telephone: 01308 423254.

● **HOW TO GET THERE:** Eype is about ½ mile south of the A35 Bridport bypass. Leave the A35, following the sign for Eype, pass the picnic area and turn left, signed 'Eype's Mouth'. After only a few yards turn right again, signed 'Eype's Mouth'. When the road divides take the right-hand road, signed for the New Inn. The road runs downhill to the inn, which is on the right.

● **PARKING:** The New Inn's car park, in front of the pub.

● **LENGTH OF THE WALK:** 2½ miles. Hilly but no steep climbs. Map: OS Landranger 193 Taunton and Lyme Regis (inn GR 449917).

THE WALK

With your back to the front of the inn, walk down the road past attractive cottages. Leave the road as it turns left and keep straight on along a wide path with a wall on the right. After about 50 yards turn right down a narrow footpath which is sunk deep between banks crowned with hazels. The path descends to cross a stream. Follow the path as it turns left a little uphill to a stile. Cross the stile to emerge onto an open, grassy hillside. Turn right to walk up the hill with a hedge close on your right. All around you are green, curving hills, dipping to give a glimpse of the sea at Eype's Mouth. At the top of the field you will see an iron gate on the right. Turn right through the gate. Keep straight on following the path up the field ahead to another gate. Go through the gate and cross the field towards the corner of a fence. Walk up the field with the fence close on your right. Aim for the modern, centrally placed house which you will see near Down House Farm on the hillside ahead. Grey farm buildings stand to the left of the house and an older house is on the right. Climb the stile ahead which brings

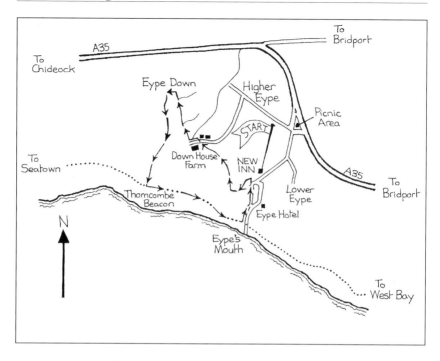

you to a lane directly in front of the central house.

Turn left along the lane past Down House Farm on the left and continue to a footpath sign. Several paths are indicated here. Turn hard right up the track signed for Eype Down. The track winds uphill through coppiced woodlands, carpeted in season with drifts of bluebells, red campion and wild garlic. Tunnels in the soft earth betray the presence of foxes and badgers. The track bears left past a grassy path on the right to follow a terraced way along the open hillside and rise to the top of Eype Down. Keep to the same track as it turns left to an open grassy area. Bear left for a few yards to a signpost, then turn sharp left signed for the Coast Path and Thorncombe Beacon. Now you will see Thorncombe Beacon against the skyline a little to your right. Pause here to enjoy one of the finest views in Dorset. The little town of Bridport lies to the east, tucked snugly in the valley of the river Brit, sheltered by Eggardon Hill which is crowned with the embankments of one of the county's most impressive hill forts. To the west is Golden Cap, outlined against the great sweep of Lyme Bay.

Follow the path as it dips to a gate. Go through the gate and follow the downland ridge, keeping a hedge on your left, towards

Thorncombe Beacon. Cross the stile just before the grassy slope leading up to the beacon and walk straight ahead to meet the Coast Path which runs past it. Turn left.

 Coast Path walkers join the walk at this point. Follow the clifftop path as it descends to a stile and continues over a field towards Eype's Mouth. Ahead you will see the pier of Bridport's tiny harbour, West Bay, sandwiched between sheer sandstone cliffs, and, beyond, the low arc of the Chesil Beach. Follow the Coast Path as the signposts direct to descend to the beach at Eype's Mouth.

Turn left up the lane past the post office. The lane leads over a stream and a few yards past this point look carefully for some steps leading to a narrow path on the left. Follow this attractive path to rejoin the lane just below the New Inn.

THORNCOMBE BEACON TO THE BRIDE RIVER BRIDGE (3½ MILES)

Follow Walk 4 as far as Eype's Mouth. Bear right in Eype's Mouth to descend the steps and cross the stream. Follow the Coast Path up the hill ahead and along the clifftop. The path swings inland a little before returning to the cliff to give a view of West Bay. At the time of writing the Coast Path has been diverted at this point. If the diversion still applies follow the notices directing you to turn left beside a field to meet a road. Turn right downhill, then left to cross the bridge over West Bay harbour. Once a busy trading post, this tiny harbour is now a colourful scene with fishing boats rocking gently beside the quay. Turn left past St John's church, then right just past the Seagulls' restaurant, following the Coast Path sign. A steep climb brings you to the top of East Cliff. The path traces the cliff edge with golf links on the left, dips round an inlet and continues to a large stone at the junction of two paths. Turn right to descend the cliff to the beach in front of the large caravan site at Burton Freshwater. Turn left to walk along the embankment in front of the caravans. Bear left, then right following the yellow footpath signs, to pass the caravan park office. A track brings you to a gate. Go through the gate and turn left to a junction of several paths. Turn right, then take the second track on the left round the field to cross a stile. Cross the meadow ahead, signed 'Burton Bradstock, and Abbotsbury'. Over the next meadow turn right, signed 'Burton Bradstock', to cross the bridge over the river Bride.

BURTON BRADSTOCK
The Three Horseshoes Inn

*D*orset *scenery at its most beguiling can be enjoyed on this easy walk. After a clifftop ramble the route turns inland to follow the river Bride to Burton Bradstock, one of the county's most enchanting villages. Before returning, there is a magnificent view from the crest of North Hill over the valley of the Bride.*

The Three Horseshoes has stood on the corner of Mill Lane in Burton Bradstock, facing south over water meadows threaded by the river Bride, for over 350 years. Long, low, built of pale golden stone beneath a darkly thatched roof, it must be everyone's idea of a traditional Dorset pub. The landlord and his wife love their charming home and after sampling their warm hospitality and delicious food I am sure you will too! Warm log fires greet you in the oak-beamed bar on colder days and the walls are hung with a fascinating array of pictures showing the village in former times. You will discover more of these delightful scenes from the past in the separate non-smoking restaurant. This, the oldest part of the inn, has the atmosphere of a country cottage with frilled curtains at the windows and comfortable window seats.

The bar and restaurant menus are varied and interesting, using fresh local produce whenever possible. Among the home-cooked dishes you will find Dorset specialities such as Ham Shank glazed with honey and 'Dorset Fat Horses' – a mouth-watering terrine of minced pork, chicken and crab flavoured with herbs and chillies. Fish comes straight from the boats. Game dishes are also a feature of the menu. Real ales include Palmers Tally Ho! 200, IPA, and Copper, a pleasant light ale. There is an extensive wine list from around the world, and two ciders.

The pub is open from 11 am to 11 pm, 12 noon to 10.30 pm on Sundays and meals are served from 12 noon to 2 pm and from 6 pm to 9 pm. There is a family room and a sunny garden with a children's play area. Telephone: 01308 897259

● **HOW TO GET THERE:** Approaching from the west, take the B3157 from Bridport. Drive into Burton Bradstock village past the Anchor inn to the Three Horseshoes which is on your left. Approaching from the east along the A35 turn left along the second road signed for Shipton Gorge. Drive through that village and keep straight ahead to meet the B3157 in Burton Bradstock. Turn left and the pub is on your left.

● **PARKING:** In the pub car park opposite the front of the pub. Turn left into Mill Lane then immediately right into the car park. The landlord is happy for patrons to leave cars while they walk but have a word with one of the staff first.

● **LENGTH OF THE WALK:** 4½ miles. Maps: OS Landranger 193 Taunton and Lyme Regis and 194 Dorchester, Weymouth (inn GR 488894).

THE WALK

Turn right from the front of the pub to the corner of Mill Lane to meet the B3157. Turn left past the bus shelter on your right and follow the road to the point where it curves sharply left. Leave the B3157 at this point and bear right along a lane. The river runs through meadows on the right. Keep ahead, following the sign 'To Coast Path West'. The lane becomes a grassy track leading to a stile. Cross this and walk over the meadow ahead with the river Bride running close on your right. At the next signpost you will see a bridge over the Bride and at this point the walk joins the Coast Path.

● Follow the sign for Burton Beach. Cross the stile and turn left, following the sign for Hive Beach. An easy climb brings you to the top of Burton Cliff, which drops a vertical 100 ft to the beach below. Follow the grassy clifftop path past a footpath sign for Burton Bradstock. Keep ahead until you see a lane on the left. Do not cross

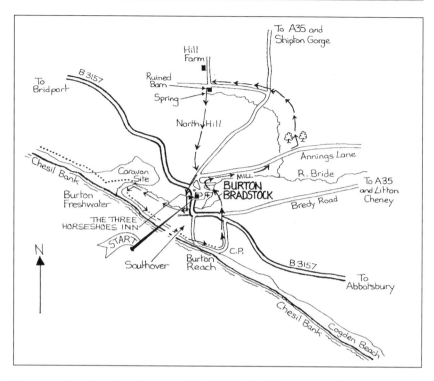

the wooden barrier close to the cliff edge but turn a little inland to continue, with the lane now running parallel on the left, towards the Burton Cliff Hotel. Opposite the hotel, descend the steps to Burton (locally called Hive) Beach. Here the Dorset coastline changes as sandstone cliffs give way to low clay bluffs fringing the great curve of the Chesil Bank. A beach café serves snacks and light meals.

Turn left up the road leading away from the beach to pass the café on your left. When the road meets the B3157, turn left for a few yards, then cross and follow the footpath sign 'To the Village'. An attractive path leads over two stone stiles to a lane. Cross the lane and go over the wooden stile ahead into a meadow. The cottages of Burton Bradstock and the church's 15th-century tower lie over the fields on your left. Keep straight ahead to cross a bridge and take the pretty streamside path to the church, around which a maze of narrow lanes winds between creeper-covered thatched cottages built of pale gold stone. Leaflets are available inside the church with a map to help you explore the village.

The walk continues down Darby Lane, opposite the church. At the end of the lane, turn right along Grove Road leading to the riverside. On the left you will see 18th-century Grove House which once manufactured linens and sailcloth. Before the trade passed to Bridport, Burton Bradstock had three mills processing locally-grown flax and hemp. A little further along the lane is a flax swingling mill, now flats. An inscription states that the mill was built by Richard Roberts in 1803. To 'swingle' flax was to dress it by breaking down the non-fibrous parts of flax stems. The soft stems could then be drawn into long strands to make linen. Follow the riverside path to a lane. Bear right a little to continue along the lane past a farm and uphill to a small wood on the left. Just before the end of the wood turn left through a gate to follow a sunken bridleway leading through the trees. The path rises to emerge onto open grassland. Keep ahead to go through a gate and continue up the field with a hedge on your right. Go through the next gate and turn immediately left to walk towards some houses with a hedge on your left. Leave the field through a gate leading to a lane running between the houses to a road. Turn left along the road for a few yards then take the first lane on the right. Walk up the lane until you come to the turning for Hill Farm on the right. Opposite is the stone wall of a ruined barn. Turn left through the gate just past the wall of the barn and walk straight ahead down the field. (The bridleway may be obscured.) Continue up the next field with the hedge on your left. At the top of the rise you come to a small wooden gate. Now you are rewarded by the splendid view from the crest of North Hill. Go through the gate and walk down the field to continue down a sunken bridleway to a lane. Follow the lane to the road in Burton Bradstock. Bear a little right along the road to leave a green on your left and continue to the B3157. Turn left to walk down the road to The Three Horseshoes and your car.

THE BRIDE RIVER BRIDGE TO THE FOOTBRIDGE ONTO CHESIL BANK ($3^1/_4$ MILES)

Follow Walk 5 to Burton Beach. When the walk turns left keep straight on, leaving the car park on your left, to climb the cliff. Pass to the seaward side of the caravans and follow the path down to the Chesil Bank at Cogden Beach. Keep ahead along a pleasant path beside the shingle and turn left for a few yards then right as indicated to pass Burton Mere on your right. Continue with a hedge on your right to a wooden footbridge on the right. Turn right over the bridge, then left along the Chesil Bank.

SWYRE
The Bull

Although this superb walk includes a rather demanding ³/₄ mile along the Chesil Bank I think you will feel amply rewarded by the wildlife on the mere and in summer by the wealth of flowering plants the Bank supports. The walk climbs over the South Dorset Ridgeway to give splendid views and visits another of Dorset's timeless villages, Puncknowle, before returning to Swyre.

Swyre is a scattering of grey stone farms and cottages tucked in a dip of the downs, with lanes running down to the Chesil Bank only a little more than ¹/₂ mile away. In common with most south coast villages, the smuggling of wines, spirits and luxury goods from France was the local industry during the 18th and 19th centuries and the men from Swyre seem to have been particularly busy! To find out more and discover what happened to them when they were caught and brought before the magistrates at the Quarter Sessions you must call at the Bull, which preserves documents from those times. There has been a hostelry on the site since 1795 when it was originally a cider house. Now the Bull is a handsome, Victorian-style building with plenty of room for its many patrons. Red plush seating and comfortable Windsor chairs in the bar and cosy dining room contribute to its welcoming atmosphere.

Good, substantial home-made food is available from 12 noon to 2 pm and 6 pm to 9.30 pm. Popular choices include a succulent lasagne and a rich moussaka. There are also several fish dishes, such as Plaice Paris with prawn and mushroom sauce. Among the real ales are 6X and Speckled Hen and the ciders available are Scrumpy Jack and Addlestone's Cask Conditioned. Drinking hours are until 11 in the evening.

Dogs are welcome in the bar. As the pub does get busy the landlord requests that you let him know if you intend to leave your car before your walk. Telephone: 01308 897250.

- **HOW TO GET THERE:** Swyre is beside the coast road, the B3157, about 5 miles east of Bridport. The Bull overlooks the road.
- **PARKING:** In the Bull's car park.
- **LENGTH OF THE WALK:** 4$\frac{1}{2}$ miles. As this walk includes a short section along the loose gravel of the Chesil Bank allow extra time and wear strong shoes. Map: OS Landranger 194 Dorchester, Weymouth and surrounding area (inn GR 528882).

THE WALK

Leave the front of the Bull on your right and walk down the road. You will see the church a few yards down a lane on the right. Pass the lane to the church and turn left just past the war memorial, following the footpath sign 'To the Beach'. Go through the gate and continue down the field. Through the next gate there is a signpost where a path joins on the left. Do not take it but keep ahead, following the sign 'To Beach'. (The other path is signed 'To Beach, floods in winter' and is the route marked on the OS map. However, our path, though not indicated on the map, is a marked footpath and safer.) Continue with the hedge on your left for about 200 yards and bear left a little through a gap in the hedge. Keep ahead with the hedge on your left through another gap in an adjoining hedge. The Chesil Bank and the mere are directly ahead. Continue with the hedge still on your left to a small stile marked with a yellow arrow footpath sign. Cross the stile to reach the grassy

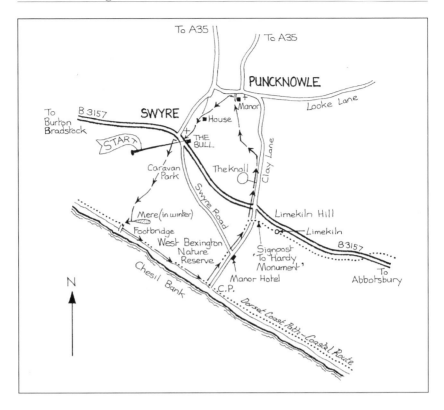

shores of the mere. Turn right to walk round the shore to meet the Coastal Path at a footbridge and stile giving access to the Chesil Bank.

The Chesil Bank is one of the geological wonders of the world. This great Bank or Beach of graded pebbles created by the force of Atlantic currents runs for 18 miles from West Bay to the Isle of Portland. The pebbles range from pea-gravel in the west to large rocks in the east. The Bank's treacherous undertow which has proved fatal for many ships driven onto its lee shore makes it unsuitable for bathing. And it is surprising how many flowers flourish in its inhospitable crannies – in summer it is colourful with white sea campion, yellow horned sea poppies and crinkly-leaved sea kale.

Bear left from the stile to walk over the pebbles with the mere on your left. The eastern end of the mere is blocked with dense rushes, home for warblers and water rails. The going improves as you near the road leading uphill from the car park at West Bexington. Turn left up the road, following the inland route of the Coast Path. Pass the

Manor Hotel and when the road bears left keep straight on up a track signed for the Hardy Monument. The track climbs up Limekiln Hill to a signpost indicating a path on the right to the Hardy Monument.

Leave the Coast Path, which turns right, and keep straight on to the road, the B3157, which at this point runs parallel with the South Dorset Ridgeway. Pause to enjoy the magnificent view seaward over the coastal plain to the waters of the Fleet, the largest tidal lagoon in Britain, trapped behind the Chesil Bank. Cross straight over the road and follow Clay Lane ahead. This rises to give wonderful views inland over gently curving hills and valleys dotted with small woods sheltering picturesque farms and villages. A short footpath on the left leads to the top of The Knoll, crowned with its old coastguards' lookout. Follow the lane to a footpath sign on the left, 'Puncknowle ½'. Turn left as the sign directs and continue through a gate in front of some farm buildings. Turn right, following the sign for Puncknowle, over a stile and continue downhill over stiles and through gates. A path through tree-shaded glades leads to a lane which descends into Puncknowle village. Our way is left here but turn right for a few steps to enjoy the village. Puncknowle (pronounced 'Punnel') seems as remote from the 20th century as Mars! Tall chestnut trees noisy with cawing rooks shelter a tiny Norman church and an ancient manor. Opposite, a long row of thatched houses include the 16th-century Crown Inn, featured in Walk 7.

To continue the walk, turn left from the lane end as directed above and a few yards further on turn left, following the footpath sign for Swyre and the Bull. Pass a house on the left and continue between fences to cross a stile. The path now runs half-right, diagonally over the field. If the path is not clear, make first for the corner of a hedge you will see projecting over the field, then for the house you will see beyond it. The path meets a lane by the house. Bear left past the house to walk down the footpath ahead to the Bull, which is on the left.

 FOOTBRIDGE TO CHESIL BANK TO LIMEKILN HILL (1½ MILES)

Follow Walk 6 as far as the turning on Limekiln Hill for the Hardy Monument.

 COASTAL ROUTE – WEST BEXINGTON TO OSMINGTON MILLS (22½ MILES)

In order to include a wider variety of scenery the Dorset Coast Path offers a choice of routes from the beach at West Bexington. You may prefer to follow the coastal route of the Coast Path, which offers the quiet waters of the Fleet and Abbotsbury with its famous Swannery. Those choosing the circular routes also have an opportunity to visit Abbotsbury (see Walk 8). Walking round Weymouth can be tiring but you are never out of sight of the sea. After a distance of little over 22 miles the coastal route joins the inland route just north of Osmington Mills (see Walk 13).

 ### WEST BEXINGTON TO ABBOTSBURY (3½ MILES)

If you wish to take the coastal route follow the route of Walk 6 from the footbridge onto the Chesil Bank to the beach at West Bexington. Continue straight ahead to follow the track beside the Bank. It is pleasant walking, accompanied by the soft thud of the waves on the shingle. On the left a long, low swell of downland shelters lonely farms and cottages. The Path passes a row of weatherboarded coastguard cottages and continues to the car park at Abbotsbury beach (refreshments available). Keep the car park on your left and follow the path as it curves left between hillsides scored with strip lynchets. The tiny chapel of St Catherine crowns Chapel Hill on the right.

Pass a footpath sign on the right and keep ahead to a signpost. Here you have a choice of routes. The Coast Path turns right over the stile to skirt Chapel Hill. But if you would like to visit Abbotsbury keep straight ahead. The track divides twice. On each occasion take the right-hand path to emerge in the village near the post office.

To keep to the Coast Path turn right as directed to follow a very narrow path round Chapel Hill. Just past a marker stone bear left over a stile by a gate leading into woodland (not the gate directly ahead). Leave the wood to continue along a field edge. Beyond a stone wall on the right you have a fine view of Abbotsbury. Look for a signpost in front of the wall and turn right down the bank to cross a stream to reach it. You can turn left here to walk into Abbotsbury but to continue along the Coast Path turn right, signed 'Swannery and Weymouth'.

 ### ABBOTSBURY TO RODDEN HIVE (2½ MILES)

Continue through a wooded area and climb a stone stile on the left to meet a lane to the Swannery. Turn right, pass the entrance to the Swannery, and follow the lane as it curves left to a road. Turn right down the road to Horsepool Farm. When the road bends right climb up to a stile straight ahead, cross, and continue up the side of a field. Cross a stile on the left and continue uphill to a signpost. Bear right to a marker post on top of the hill and follow the ridge for a mile over stiles then turn right as the sign directs, downhill beside the eastern fringe of Hodder's Coppice. Signs then direct you left, hedge on left, to continue straight over a lane. Keep ahead up the side of a field. The path bears right, then turns to follow the eastern edge of Wyke Wood, which is on your right. The Fleet and Chesil Bank are now directly ahead. Cross a stone bridge and turn left over meadows past a footpath to Langton Herring on the left. The path leads to a gate on the left. Go through, turn right and follow field paths to the Fleet shore at Rodden Hive.

 RODDEN HIVE TO EAST FLEET (3 MILES)

Follow the well-signed shore path beside the Fleet to the slipway at Langton Hive Point. Follow the signs for East Fleet. After about ½ mile you come to a junction of paths. Turn right, keeping a wall on your left, to cross a small peninsula and return to the Fleet shore close to the Moonfleet Manor Hotel. A large sign says 'Walkers Welcome' and excellent refreshments are available.

 EAST FLEET TO FERRY BRIDGE (4 MILES)

Continue along the Coast Path beside the Fleet with a hedge on your right past East Fleet campsite. When you reach the sentry box at the entrance to the Chickerell Rifle Ranges look to see if a red flag is flying. If so, you must wait to be escorted across by the sentry when it is safe to do so. Otherwise follow the signs, keeping to the right of the marker posts. Follow the signs for Weymouth, passing to the seaward side of the caravans in the Littlesea Holiday Park. Just past the last of the caravans the path bears half-right diagonally up the side of a grassy slope to a signpost a little to your right. Follow the path as it tunnels through the bushes before emerging in the open to bear right along the edge of a field. The path leads round the Royal Engineers Bridging Camp. Turn right down the access road then left to continue through meadows. Walk round the sands of Pirate Cove and bear right up the cliff. Walk through Blue Waters caravan site, keeping as close to the coast as possible, descend the steps to the beach and walk to meet the main road, the A354, at Ferry Bridge, which crosses Small Mouth, the entrance to the Fleet.

FERRY BRIDGE TO OSMINGTON MILLS (9½ MILES) No acorn symbols until Redcliff Point.

Cross the A354 and follow the footpath sign opposite the Ferry Bridge Inn. The path bears left to follow the western edge of Portland Harbour. Ignore the obvious track of the former railway and keep to the clifftop to meet Old Castle Road just past the Sailing Centre. Walk up the road past the ruins of Sandsfoot Castle on the right and turn right, following the public footpath sign. The path runs past Castle Cove through the trees of the Western Ledges past the northern breakwater. Keep ahead to pass the lookout post on the left and follow the lane to Nothe Fort on the headland (open to the public). Pass to the left of the fort and bear left. From here there is a splendid view over Weymouth. Descend the first flight of steps on the right to the harbour and take the ferry across (small charge). Now follow Weymouth sea front and continue along the sea wall as far as the Oasis Café. Here the main road, the A353, turns left.

Keep straight ahead up the minor road, Bowleaze Cove Road, to descend to Bowleaze Cove on the right. Continue along Bowleaze Cove Road to go through two gates and follow a wide track leading uphill. About 50 yards from the top of the hill, bear half-right diagonally along a grassy path to a stile. Cross and take the wide path to Redcliff Point.

Follow the good path, now marked with Coast Path acorns, as it traces the clifftop and runs to the right of Osmington Bay Holiday Centre. Boardwalks take you over marshy areas before the path rises above the landslips to follow the clifftop above Black Head. Follow the signs to meet the inland route of the Coast Path just north of Osmington Mills. Turn right to walk down to the Smugglers Inn. Now follow the directions in Walk 13.

PUNCKNOWLE
The Crown Inn
<SYMBOL>

Magnificent views over the coast and inland can be enjoyed throughout this walk. The route follows the Bronze Age track, now the South Dorset Ridgeway, for over a mile before turning inland close to Abbotsbury hill fort and returning to the Bride valley along peaceful country lanes.

Puncknowle (call it Punnel), tucked snugly in the valley of the river Bride, must be most people's idea of a typical English village. Chestnut trees shade a small church with a Norman tower overlooking an ancient manor house with smoothly manicured lawns. And, as you might expect, opposite the manor gates is a thatched pub fitting the picture perfectly with its dark beams, deep window seats and huge fireplaces. The Crown Inn offers the traditional peaceful atmosphere of a Dorset pub but there is no need to worry if you arrive with small children as there is a special family room and a delightful garden with views of the Bride valley. Most of the food is home-made with a pleasantly alcoholic bias, for example beef, raisin and ginger casserole cooked in Madeira, steak and kidney pie cooked in Palmers Tally Ho! and lamb and cranberry casserole cooked in damson wine. As well as Tally Ho!, Palmers IPA, Bridport Bitter and 200 are on offer. Taunton Traditional cider and wines, including a French house wine and a special for each month, are available.

Meals are served from 12 noon to 2 pm (2.30 pm on Sunday) and 7 pm to 9.30 pm and drinking hours are until 11 in the evening. Dogs are welcome in the bar areas. The Crown does get busy so have a word with the landlord if you intend to leave your car while you walk. For a longer stay the Crown offers very reasonably priced accommodation. Telephone: 01308 897711.

● **HOW TO GET THERE:** Puncknowle is a little off the beaten track but well worth finding. The best approach is off the B3157, the coast road between Bridport and Abbotsbury. Turn off the B3157 for Puncknowle in Swyre and in less than 1/2 mile turn right into Puncknowle village. The Crown Inn is on the left, almost opposite the church. The entrance to the car park is just past the inn on the left.

● **PARKING:** In the Crown Inn's car park or, if it is full, there is roadside parking.

● **LENGTH OF THE WALK:** 5 1/2 miles. Easy walking. Map: OS Landranger 194 Dorchester, Weymouth and surrounding area (inn GR 535887).

THE WALK

Before starting this walk find time to visit the church, almost opposite the pub. It is full of interest with a fine 12th-century chancel arch surmounted by the remains of medieval wall paintings. The massive entrance door in the north wall dates from the 17th century and bears nail studs forming the initials R. N. for Robert Napier. The Napier family were lords of the manor during the 17th century and from the churchyard you can glimpse the charming manor house described by Frederick Treves in *Highways and Byways in Dorset* as 'a marvel of ancient dignity and peace'.

Turn left in front of the Crown to leave the church and the gates of the manor on your right. Continue past the row of cottages to the junction of Looke Lane and Clay Lane. Do not take either lane but turn right up the farm entrance opposite Looke Lane. Walk past the farm buildings, and two further barns on the left, and keep to the track as it climbs gently to meet Clay Lane. Already wide views over the Bride

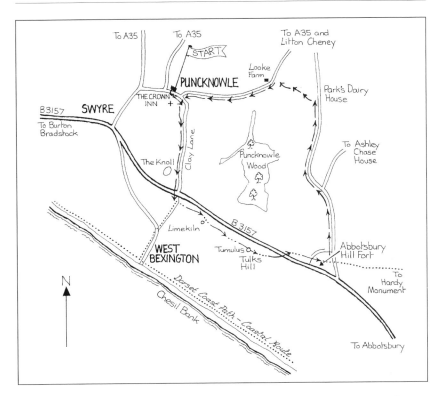

valley and surrounding downland unfold around you. Bear right up
Clay Lane. As you near the crest of the down you will see a small hill,
The Knoll, on the right. It is crowned by a former coastguards' lookout
and if you would like to enjoy their splendid view take the footpath on
the right which leads the short distance to the top.

Clay Lane then dips to meet the road, the B3157, at Limekiln Hill.
Cross over and walk down the partly grassed, cobbled track ahead to a
joining path on the left, signed 'Hardy Monument'.

● Turn left to join the Coast Path, which follows the South Dorset
Ridgeway. The track rises to the road. With the road on your left
climb the stile ahead, signed 'Hardy Monument', to emerge on the green
slopes of Limekiln Hill. The path is not clear but keep ahead with the thick
bramble, gorse and hawthorn scrub on your right. (Ignore any tracks
leading down through the bushes.) The National Trust has restored the
limekiln which gives the hillside its name and after about ½ mile you will
see the low walls surrounding the top of the kiln with an iron grid over the
central well a few yards down the hill on your right (GR 540870).

Continue along the ridge and as you approach a thicket of bushes and small trees a wooden post indicates the path through them. Climb the stone steps over a wall and, bearing a little left, walk up the hill to continue with the road about 50 yards away on the left. The path becomes clearer as it runs closer to the road towards the prominent mound – a Bronze Age burial site or tumulus – crowning Tulks Hill. When you have followed the path to the top of the hill the view is one of the finest in the county. As you look seaward the Dorset coastline is revealed from Portland in the east to Start Point beyond Lyme Bay in the west. Inland, rolling downland rises to the county's highest hills, Eggardon, Pilsdon Pen and Lewesdon.

Follow the path to the road, cross, and continue along the Coast Path, signed 'Hardy Monument'. Abbotsbury Iron Age hill fort is directly ahead. At the foot of the lower embankment walk over a crosstrack and take the right-hand of the two paths ahead to climb the side of the hill fort. Follow the path as it leads across the top, dipping over the remains of embankments dug over 2,000 years ago by Celtic tribes. You pass a trig point to approach a stile in front of a beacon. Cross and walk down to a lane.

Leave the Coast Path, which continues ahead, and turn left to follow the lane towards the Bride valley. After about 1/2 mile a track joins on the left. Turn left and follow this track. Litton Cheney village is on the hillside directly ahead. The track drops steeply in front of a farm (Park's Dairy House). Turn left before the farm through a gate, leaving all the farm buildings on your right. Cross the field ahead to go through a gate and continue along the edge of a field with a hedge on the left. Bear right a little round the end of the field to go through a gate on the left and keep ahead through another gate to Looke Lane opposite Looke Farm. Turn left for a few yards then right, following the sign for Puncknowle over the farmyard to rejoin Looke Lane. Ignore the track signed 'Tulks Hill' and follow Looke Lane along the Bride valley for about 3/4 mile to the junction with Clay Lane in Puncknowle. Bear right through the village to return to the Crown.

 LIMEKILN HILL TO WHITE HILL (3 MILES)

Follow Walk 7 to the lane just past Abbotsbury Hill Fort. Cross straight over the lane, climb the stile and follow the path ahead along the Ridgeway. Continue for about a mile to cross a stile and join the route of Walk 8 by the signpost at the top of White Hill.

ABBOTSBURY
The Ilchester Arms

Two of Dorset's most charming villages are included in this walk, Abbotsbury and Portesham. The climb up to the Ridgeway is rewarded by splendid views of the Fleet and the Chesil Bank curving round the coast to Portland. A gentle stroll along the disused track of the railway that once linked Abbotsbury with Upwey completes the circuit.

Abbotsbury is a beautiful village, dark-thatched and built of rich golden stone, set snugly in a hollow of the coastal downs at the western end of the sheltered waters of the Fleet. Approving of its mild climate and rich soils, Benedictine monks founded an Abbey here in the 14th century. Among the remains of the Abbey is a massive tithe barn and the chapel of St Catherine on the top of Chapel Hill. The monks established a swannery in the reedy shores of the Fleet, which after 600 years still flourishes under the protection of the Strangways family.

The Ilchester Arms is a former coaching inn dating back 300 years with a particularly restful and welcoming atmosphere. Behind a Georgian façade you will find the heavily beamed ceilings and oak panelled window seats of an earlier age but delightful modern features include a sunny conservatory. The inn is open in summer from 11 am to 11 pm and at other times from 11 am to 3 pm (11.30 am on Mondays) and 6 pm to 11 pm. Real ales are Bass, 6X and Flowers. The menu includes tempting salads and home-made pies. Daily specials feature such delights as roast pork with mushroom sauce, Chicken Wellington with a mild mustard sauce and salmon and prawn pancakes.

The inn has a no-smoking area and dogs are welcome in the garden. If you intend to leave your car while you walk, have a word with one of the staff first. The Ilchester Arms offers excellent overnight accommodation too. Telephone: 01305 871243.

- **HOW TO GET THERE:** Abbotsbury lies beside the B3157, about 8 miles west of Weymouth. Approaching from the east, drive through the village to a T-junction and follow the B3157 as it turns right, signed for Bridport. After only a few yards be ready to turn sharp left under the arched entrance to the Ilchester Arms' car park, just before the pillared entrance to the inn. Approaching from the west, drive into the village and turn right into the car park just past the entrance to the inn.

- **PARKING:** In the inn's car park or one of the well-signed car parks in the village.

- **LENGTH OF THE WALK:** 5 miles. One fairly steep climb, otherwise easy. Map: OS Landranger 194 Dorchester, Weymouth and surrounding area (inn GR 577854).

THE WALK

With your back to the entrance to the Ilchester Arms, cross the road, bear left for a few yards, then turn right up the lane past the Old School House gift shop. Continue for about 300 yards then turn left up the track just before Spring Cottage. There is a small thatched barn on your right and a stone marked 'White Hill'. The path bears left then turns right uphill, tunnelling beneath holm oaks wreathed in honeysuckle. The path leads through a gate to climb open downland and now you enjoy wonderful views over Abbotsbury cupped in the hills, dominated by the 15th-century tower of St Nicholas' church and the dark outline of the tithe barn. The curving downland surrounding the village is scored by terraces, medieval strip lynchets, created by land-hungry farmers in

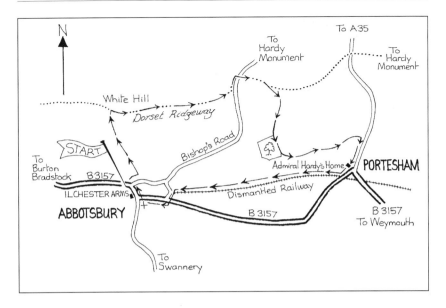

the 13th century. Keep straight on uphill, through the next gate and take the path ahead, which curves a little left to meet the Ridgeway by the signpost at the top of White Hill. Turn right, signed 'Hardy Monument', to continue along the Coast Path, which follows the Ridgeway.

Pass a sign for Abbotsbury and continue ahead to the left of some thorn bushes. Go though a gate, following the footpath sign for the Hardy Monument, with a fence on your right. After about 50 yards leave the fence and take the narrow path that bears left a little, gently uphill. (This looks unlikely but it is the correct route!) After about ½ mile turn left at the next signpost for the Hardy Monument. Skirt the field to go through a gate by a sign indicating the Ridgeway Inland Route to a lane, the Bishop's Road. Turn left along the lane for a few yards then turn right through a gate by another signpost. The path leads ahead round the rim of a bowl-shaped valley. Follow the path, keeping a fence close on the left. After about ½ mile, as you round the other side of the valley, you will see a white marker stone indicating a continuation of the Ridgeway and a path to Portesham.

Leave the Coast Path here and turn right for Portesham as indicated by the blue bridleway arrow. The path follows the valley rim a little further then drops downhill with a fence on the left. When you come to a corner follow the fence round to the right and, keeping the fence still

43

on the left, continue for about 50 yards. Now bear left, still following the fence downhill in the direction of a small wood. Above the wood the hillside drops abruptly at your feet too steeply to descend. But our way is through the gate you will see at the foot of the hill in front of the wood. A blue arrow bridleway sign on a gatepost on your left solves our problem! Turn right as the sign directs to descend gradually for about 100 yards, then turn left to go through the gate and follow the path along a small valley with the wood on your right. When the wood ends bear a little left through a gate and continue, with a hedge on your right. Cross a lane through two gates and at the end of the field bear right as a sign indicates towards Portesham village. After about ¼ mile look for a stile on the right. Turn right over the stile to a road. Turn left and after about 30 yards turn right down New Road to the main road through Portesham, the B3157. Turn right in the direction of Abbotsbury. You pass a grey stone house on the right with a pillared porch surmounted by two stone lions. This was the boyhood home of Admiral Sir Thomas Masterman Hardy who commanded Nelson's flagship *Victory* at the battle of Trafalgar.

Continue beside the Abbotsbury road for about 100 yards then turn right up the track just past the Millmead Country Hotel. Keep ahead for about 30 yards, then, leaving a group of farm buildings on the left, go through the gate a little to your right which leads up to the track of the former railway. A pleasant mile-long walk along the track leads back to the B3157 in Abbotsbury. Turn right when you reach the road to walk through the village, turning right at the T-junction to the Ilchester Arms.

 ### WHITE HILL TO BLACK DOWN BARN (2¾ MILES)

From White Hill follow the route of Walk 8 as far as the marker post indicating the right turn to Portesham. Bear left a little as indicated by the yellow arrow and climb the steps to cross a stile. Continue, with the hedge on the left, and just before the next gate you will see a small stone circle dating from around 1800 BC on the right. The path dips through gates to a road. Turn left along the road for a few yards then turn right, following the footpath sign for the Hardy Monument. As the path descends to Black Down Barn you may wish to make a short detour along a footpath on the right to visit a reconstructed Neolithic dolmen, the Hell Stone. In the valley join the route of Walk 9 by turning left at the first signpost for the Hardy Monument.

PORTESHAM
The Kings Arms

The magnificent view from the Hardy Monument on the top of Black Down Hill is an outstanding feature of this walk. It also includes one of the most spectacular stretches of the South Dorset Ridgeway along the crest of Bronkham Hill.

Portesham is a neat, compact village built of dove-grey stone with many old-world thatched houses. Rising 780 ft north of the village is Black Down Hill, crowned by the tall, chimney-shaped monument commemorating Portesham's most famous former resident, Admiral Sir Thomas Masterman Hardy, captain of Nelson's flagship *Victory* at the battle of Trafalgar. This nautical theme is very much a feature of the village pub, the Kings Arms. From the windows you can see the house where the captain spent his boyhood and part of the spacious bar area beside the main entrance was designed as a replica of his cabin on board the *Victory*. This includes a false skylight painted with stars in the ceiling. The captain liked to imagine he could see the sky! A more homely touch is provided by a collection of over 200 teapots.

Two real ales are always on offer, one of which is Flowers Original. Appetising home-cooked dishes include chicken and mushroom pie, curries and local ham. There is a range of vegetarian dishes and a special menu for children. Families are well cared for – inside there is a family room and a safe play area can be found outside in the attractive garden. Dogs are welcome on leads in the garden. Opening times are from 11 am to 11 pm in the summer, and at other times the hours are Monday to Saturday 11 am to 2.30 pm and 6.30 pm to 11 pm, Sunday 12 noon to 3 pm and 7 pm to 10.30 pm. Telephone: 01305 871342.

- **HOW TO GET THERE:** Portesham lies beside the B3157, about 7 miles west of Weymouth. The Kings Arms is at the south end of the village on the corner where the B3157 turns left for Abbotsbury.
- **PARKING:** In the inn's car park.
- **LENGTH OF THE WALK:** 5 miles. Two fairly steep but short climbs, otherwise easy. Map: OS Landranger 194 Dorchester, Weymouth and surrounding area (inn GR 603857).

THE WALK

Turn right from the Kings Arms car park to the corner where the B3157 turns left for Abbotsbury. Across the road stands Admiral Hardy's home, a solidly built house of grey stone with two stone lions surmounting the porch. Hardy went to sea as 'captain's servant' at the age of twelve. In 1793 he was Lieutenant aboard the frigate *Meleager* where he is said to have made the acquaintance of Nelson. In 1803 he was given command of *Victory*. All his life he retained his love for Portesham which he called in local dialect 'Possum', and for all things made in Dorset, especially the mutton, cheese and beer!

Turn right again to leave the B3157 and walk up Portesham's main street, Front Street, signed for Hardy Monument. You pass the entrance to the Kings Arms on your right and the church on your left. At the top of the street a lane joins Front Street on the left. Our way is right here past the village store but first you might like to cross the road on the left to see the charming village pond. In the centre a small waterfall provides a playground for a lively mob of ducks and moorhens. Return to follow the lane past the store and turn right, following the bridleway, signed 'Hardy Monument'.

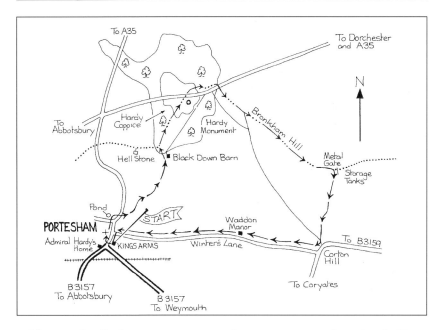

The track climbs to a gate opening onto open downland. Keep ahead uphill with the hedge on the left. Nearing the top of the rise bear right with a stone wall now on your left. Already you can look down on Portesham tucked as securely in the valley as a finger in a glove. The track turns left between stone walls then bears right with a wall on the right. Go through a gate and directly ahead on the skyline you will see the unmistakable outline of the Hardy Monument. Drop a little downhill to another gate to meet a crosstrack. Turn left to walk down into the valley at the foot of Black Down Hill. Only the walls remain of the huge Black Down Barn which you will see to the right of the path. Just past the barn ignore the obvious footpath ahead, signed for the Hardy Monument, and turn left for a few yards to another signpost. Bear right here uphill on the Coast Path following the sign 'Inland Route, Hardy Monument'. (If you would like to see the Hell Stone, a reconstructed Neolithic dolmen, you could make a detour here of about ½ mile. Do not turn right for the monument but keep straight on over a stone stile. Walk up the side of the field ahead and cross a stone stile on the left, signed for the Hell Stone. A short footpath leads to the dolmen. Return to take the path to the monument.)

After a scattering of pines, the path climbs through the oak and beech woods of Hardy Coppice. At the next signpost keep ahead for the Hardy Monument. Leave the woods to climb to the monument. The views in all directions are spectacular. Inland, rolling chalk downland reaches to the fringes of Cranborne Chase. Eastwards are the Purbeck Hills and West is the whole Dorset coast as far as Start Point in Devon. The 72 ft high tower can be climbed by a winding staircase to a platform on the top on Saturdays and Sundays during the summer.

Follow the track from the monument to the road and turn right for a few yards. The official inland route now crosses the road to take the very narrow path which winds slightly inland down to a wood before returning to the road. Bear left down the road. In the dip you will see a footpath sign on the right for the 'Inland Coast Path and Osmington. Turn right as indicated to follow a superb track along the crest of Bronkham Hill with splendid views all the way. Continue past a track on the left for Martinstown and keep straight on past the next footpath sign. As the track begins to descend more steeply you reach a metal gate. Beyond the gate are two large, white storage tanks. You need to navigate carefully at this point. Leave the Coast Path, which continues straight on, and turn right just before the gate. Pick your way along a narrow path for a few yards. Now a signpost indicates the path downhill to Corton Hill and Coryates. Cross the stile on the left and bear right downhill, hedge on the right. At the foot of the field turn right over two stiles and follow the field edge for about 30 yards. Now turn left through a gate and continue downhill to join a concrete track leading to a road. Turn right to a junction and turn right for Portesham to follow Winter's Lane back to the village past Waddon Manor which dates from the early 18th century. When the lane meets Front Street in Portesham turn left to return to the Kings Arms.

BLACK DOWN BARN TO THE TURNING FOR FRIAR WADDON (3 MILES)

Follow the route of Walk 9 from Black Down Barn to the turning for Corton and Coryates. Keep straight on through the metal gate along the Ridgeway, which descends past two burial mounds on the left. The path curves left then right through a gate to run between two large burial mounds before continuing straight ahead to meet the route of Walk 10 by the footpath sign at the turning for Friar Waddon.

UPWEY
The Old Ship Inn

ᴥ᪻ᴤ

This rewarding ramble includes two ridge walks with wonderful views, seawards over Weymouth and Portland, and inland to Dorset's most impressive hill fort, Maiden Castle. The return route follows part of the old Roman road between Dorchester and Weymouth.

Upwey is a charming grey stone village nestling in a narrow valley just north of Weymouth. As its name suggests, the houses cluster around the source of the river Wey. The spring bubbling beneath stone arches has become famous as a 'wishing well'. In earlier times it was thought that the well possessed medicinal properties and King George III often visited Upwey to drink the water while staying in Weymouth. The gold cup from which he drank is said to be the one presented at the Ascot races. The rural atmosphere of this old-world village is captured to perfection in its comfortable hostelry, the Old Ship. Like many Dorset inns, it was once a long row of low, stone-built cottages. A wide range of tempting dishes are on offer. These include delicious home-made soups, garlic mushrooms (made with field mushrooms in season!), lamb filled with forcemeat and flavoured with rosemary, and chicken stuffed with pork and herbs in white wine and mushroom sauce. Real ales are Boddingtons, Greenalls Original and Marston's Pedigree. And if you enjoy good wine you have a treat in store – there is a wine list of over 60 excellent wines with up to 14 on offer by the glass. Dogs (with well-behaved owners) are welcome. Outside you will find a pleasant patio with tables and umbrellas.

The inn is open on Monday to Friday from 11 am to 2.30 pm (to 3 pm on Saturday and from 12 pm to 3 pm for Sunday lunch) and in the evenings from 6 pm to 11 pm (Sundays 7 pm to 10.30 pm). Have a word with the management before going for your walk if you want to leave your car in the car park. Telephone: 01305 812522.

- **HOW TO GET THERE:** The Old Ship is close to the A354 about 3 miles south of Dorchester. Unfortunately, the turning to the pub is unsigned so, approaching from Dorchester, follow the signs for Weymouth for about 3 miles and pass the Weymouth Borough sign. The road bends sharp left, then right to go under a railway bridge. About 200 yards after the bridge turn right then immediately right again up a lane marked with a no-through-road sign. The Old Ship is on the left. There is limited parking in front and a small car park on the left just past the inn.
- **PARKING:** In the pub car park.
- **LENGTH OF THE WALK:** 5½ miles. Two climbs, one fairly steep, otherwise easy. Map: OS Landranger 194 Dorchester, Weymouth and surrounding area (inn GR 669849).

THE WALK

With the front of the Old Ship on your right, turn right beside the pub down Little Hill, a narrow lane running between high stone walls. At the foot, turn right for a few yards to two footpath signs. Bear left to follow a pleasant grassy path which leads over stiles along the valley with downland rising on the right. Keep ahead past a farm on the left. The path becomes a tarred track and meets the B3159 almost opposite Upwey church. Turn left for a few yards then cross the road. Ignore the lane on the right marked with a no-through-road sign and walk along the lane between the café beside the Upwey wishing well on the left and the former school, now the village hall, on the right. (The entrance to the well is through the café.) Follow the lane uphill past the church

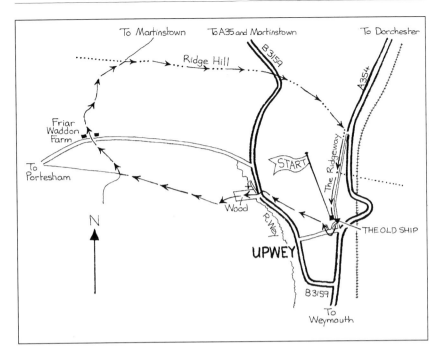

on the right. Cross a stile and climb the path through the wood ahead. As you emerge from the wood onto the open hillside there is no clear path. Bear left a little to the crest of the ridge on your left to the path that runs along the top and now bear right along the ridge. When you come to a stile marked with three footpath arrows, cross over and keep straight on along the crest of the ridge. Cross the next stile (the fence on the right meets your path at this point) and continue ahead through a gate to a narrow lane. Turn right and follow the lane to Friar Waddon Farm. Cross the road to the left of a magnificent thatched barn and walk between the farm buildings. Keep ahead over the farmyard and follow the white track ahead which bears left and zig-zags up the hillside to meet a crossing wall at the top. Turn right just before the wall and with the wall on your left follow the path to a gate on the left which opens onto the Ridgeway and the route of the Coast Path by a footpath sign indicating the Ridgeway to right and left and a path to Martinstown. Turn right to follow the Coast Path along the Ridgeway.

The track runs along the crest of Ridge Hill, giving a splendid view of the earth ramparts of Maiden Castle hill fort dominating the Winterborne valley with the rooftops of Dorchester beyond. The track

The magnificent thatched barn at Friar Waddon.

drops to cross the Martinstown road. Keep ahead, following the sign
'Inland Route East'. Just before you come to the main Dorchester-
Weymouth road, the A354, turn right, signed 'Inland Route'. At this
point the Ridgeway descends a white track, part of the original Roman
road. After about 300 yards you pass a stile on the left.

Leave the Coast Path here as it turns left over the stile, and continue
downhill to join a lane leading back to the Old Ship.

 ### TURNING FOR FRIAR WADDON TO COOMBE VALLEY ROAD (5 MILES)

Follow the route of Walk 10 as far as the stile on the left of the Roman
road. Turn left, cross the field and climb the stile to cross the A354.
Keep ahead along the track. When the track bears left keep straight on
along a grassy path which crosses a track and meets a minor road. Turn
right along the road and opposite the turning to Came Down turn right,
signed 'Bridleway for Bincombe'. The path becomes a metalled lane
which leads to a minor road. Turn left, signed 'Inland Route East', to
walk through sleepy Bincombe village. When the road turns right keep
straight on, leaving Bincombe church on your right. After about 30
yards bear left to follow a terraced path uphill. (Keep to the same path
– do not lose height.) At the top of the hill keep ahead through a gate
and follow the path as it descends to a signpost overlooking the
Coombe valley. Following the sign for Osmington Mills, cross the stile
on the right and bear left steeply downhill to the Coombe Valley Road.

SUTTON POYNTZ
The Springhead

From Sutton Poyntz, a quiet way winds up the downs past Chalbury hill fort to meet the Ridgeway. The route curves round the crest of White Horse Hill before descending towards Osmington village and returning to Sutton Poyntz over the fields. From the path you have a splendid view of the figure of George III on horseback carved out of the white chalk hillside.

Sutton Poyntz must be everyone's idea of an idyllic English village. Paths over miniature bridges lead past the mill to rows of neat cottages facing a pond overhung with willows and full of enormous fish. The village and its setting at the foot of the downs inspired many of the scenes in Thomas Hardy's novel *The Trumpet Major*. The Springhead is a large, welcoming pub in the centre of the village, overlooking the pond. Inside, the restful atmosphere is heightened by the attractive, wine-coloured decor. Among many thoughtful touches you will find flowers on every table. All the food is home-made and the Springhead's own pork sausages flavoured with garlic and coriander are highly recommended. Examples of other dishes that might be on offer are Barbary duck in cranberry and orange sauce, Texas chilli with spices and peppers, and lemon sole with parsley and lemon butter. Children are spoilt at the Springhead – if there is nothing on the menu to tempt them they can ask for a favourite dish instead! Bar snacks and salads are also obtainable. There are up to four real ales, including Flowers, as well as a range of 20 malt whiskies and an impressive wine list. Outside there is a large play area for children and a field for them to run about in. Dogs are welcome in the pub.

Opening times are Monday to Saturday from 11 am to 2.30 pm and 6 pm to 11 pm, Sunday 12 pm to 3 pm and 7 pm to 10.30 pm. Telephone: 01305 832117.

- **HOW TO GET THERE:** The turning for Sutton Poyntz village is off the A353 about 2 miles east of Weymouth. Approaching from Weymouth, turn left for Sutton Poyntz opposite the Ship Inn in Preston. In just over 1/4 mile bear right at the Y-junction in the village. The Springhead is on your right.
- **PARKING:** The Springhead has two large car parks. If these are full drive past the pub for a few yards to another car park on the left.
- **LENGTH OF THE WALK:** About 4 1/2 miles, with one gentle climb. Map: OS Landranger 194 Dorchester, Weymouth and surrounding area (inn GR 707838).

THE WALK

With the Springhead on your left and the mill pond on your right, walk along the village street to a small stone bridge. Turn right to cross the bridge then immediately left to follow a delicious narrow, shaded way beside a stream. Across the path a row of attractive cottages face the mill. The path leads down to a road. Turn left to a T-junction and turn right to walk beside the road for about 50 yards. Turn right down the delightfully named Puddledock Lane. The lane bears right then left round some houses and you will see footpath signs on the right. Turn right at the first sign and follow the track through the bushes, then keep ahead up the field path (ignore the path leading right) towards the steep slopes of Chalbury Hill.

The path curves right so that Chalbury Hill is now on your left, then bears left a little. Keep ahead with a tiny stream and hedge on your right. Follow the same path as it turns left to climb the gentle slopes at

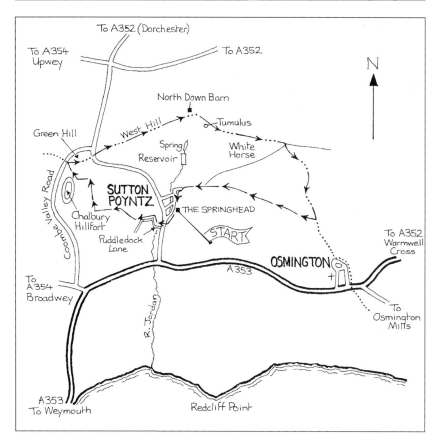

the foot of Chalbury Hill. Go through a gate and keep to the path as it bears slightly right over the field towards the Coombe Valley Road. Do not go through the gate leading to the road but turn right through another gate. Join the Coast Path Inland Route.

🢃 Turn right and follow this beautiful terraced path as it curves round the foot of Green Hill. Now on the right you have a splendid view of Chalbury Hill, one of the ancient fortified towns of Britain. Bronze Age people lived here from around 1700-500 BC and left their burial mounds and weapons. Later, in the Iron Age, Celts from Asia fortified the hilltop and cultivated the valley. You can see the low embankments separating their small fields.

The terraced path curves left as it climbs the hill. Be careful here to keep to the same terrace and not lose height. Cross the stile near the summit to a lane. Turn left for a few yards then right through a gate to follow the track signed for White Horse Hill. When the way divides take the right-hand track. The path follows the crest of West Hill giving magnificent views. In the coombe directly below you will see the reservoir which collects clear spring water from the chalk hills to supply Weymouth. Here it is filtered to remove debris and weeds. The filter is one of the funnels from Brunel's *Great Eastern* steamship, which, after an explosion on board, put into Weymouth for repairs in 1859. The funnel was removed, taken to Sutton Poyntz and has been in use ever since!

The path turns left past the ruins of Northdown Barn. In *The Trumpet Major* Thomas Hardy describes how huge military reviews, often involving two or three miles of troops, took place several times on these downs. In the novel, the barn is used as a hospital. Go through a gate and turn right to continue along the Ridgeway. When the track turns left keep straight on, signed 'Inland Route Osmington'. On the right is a large burial mound. In *The Trumpet Major* John Loveday and Anne Garland admire the view from the top, described as 'one of the most extensive in the county' reaching beyond Weymouth to Portland 'with its pebble bank, lying on the sea . . . like a great crouching animal tethered to the mainland'.

Through the next gate you may wish to take the short optional route on the right to visit the chalk figure of George III. This path rejoins our route. If not, keep ahead, following the sign for Osmington. Through the next gate turn right downhill for Osmington. Follow the path as it approaches the first houses in this attractive village.

Here the walk leaves the Coast Path, which continues straight ahead. Turn right through a gate, following the sign for Sutton Poyntz. But before taking the turning for Sutton Poyntz you may wish to see more of Osmington. It is a delightful village with many thatched cottages and an interesting church beside the ruins of a manor house. After the detour, return to the gate by the sign for Sutton Poyntz. Follow the path over the fields, bearing right over a tiny stream to go through a gate and continue over fields and stiles in the direction of Sutton Poyntz. On the hillside on the right you have a splendid view of George III covering more than an acre. The figure commemorates his many visits to Weymouth in the 18th century but unfortunately he is depicted riding *away* from the town! In *The Trumpet Major* John Loveday takes Anne Garland to see 'forty navvies at work' removing the turf to expose the chalky sub soil.

Keep straight on through gates to follow a lane past the pumping

The chalk figure of George III carved out of the down above Sutton Poyntz.

station. The lane bears left through Sutton Poyntz. Keep the stream on your right as you walk back to the Springhead, which is on your left.

 COOMBE VALLEY ROAD TO THE SUNRAY (3 MILES)

Follow the route of Walk 11 as far as the turning in Osmington for Sutton Poyntz. Keep straight on through the village and turn left, as signed, down Village Street. Turn right at the end of the road to walk up Chapel Lane to the Sunray, which is on your left just before the A353.

OSMINGTON
The Sunray
❦

A splendid clifftop ramble through the tumbled landslips above the Black Head ledges is a feature of this walk. The rocky ravines are rich in bird and plant life. The walk crosses the fields to return to Osmington past its interesting church and ruined manor.

Osmington is one of Dorset's secret villages. Busy traffic roars past on the A353 and only a few minutes away you will discover this enchanting cluster of brown-thatched houses built of locally quarried white stone. In 1816 one of our greatest landscape painters, John Constable, spent his honeymoon at the vicarage. Inspired by the beauty of his surroundings, he made a number of sketches and paintings of Osmington and the view of Weymouth Bay from the beach close by.

Osmington is a tiny village, best explored on foot, and the Sunray makes the perfect starting point. It is a large, friendly pub with a specially warm welcome for families. Outside there are well laid out grounds with a separate garden complete with a play area for families with small children. Inside, the pub is just as spacious. Screens and flowers ensure you will always find a quiet corner if you wish. Real ales are Greenalls Original, Bass, Flowers Original and a guest beer. There is a vast range of wines. Equally vast is the range of dishes on offer at the bar and in the restaurant, two examples being rack of ribs in barbecue sauce and Somerset pork chops cooked in cider with apple and mustard and cream sauce. Vegetarian dishes could include spinach and ricotta tortellini and savoury pancakes stuffed with mushrooms and cream cheese. Children have their own 'Captain Coconut' menu. In summer and at holiday times barbecues are held outside. Dogs on leads are welcome in the garden.

The Sunray is open in summer from 10 am to 11 pm and at other times from 11.30 am to 11 pm. The restaurant is open on Monday to Saturday from 12 noon to 2.30 pm, and in the evening from 5.30 pm to 10 pm (Friday and Saturday to 10.30 pm). Sunday opening is from 12 noon to 10 pm. Telephone: 01305 832148.

- **HOW TO GET THERE:** Osmington is reached from the A353 about 2 miles east of Weymouth. The Sunray is beside the road, well signed. Turn into Chapel Lane to the pub car park on the left.
- **PARKING:** In the Sunray's large car park.
- **LENGTH OF THE WALK:** 4 miles. Easy walking. Map: OS Landranger 194 Dorchester, Weymouth and surrounding area (inn GR 726829).

THE WALK

From the pub car park turn right to walk up Chapel Lane to the A353. Turn left along the pavement beside the road. Ignore the first set of yellow footpath signs on the right in front of East Farm and continue along the pavement on the other side of the road to a signpost. Turn right, signed 'Inland Route Osmington Mills'. Cross a small bridge and stile. The path is not clear, but walk straight up the field ahead, hedge on left. Cross the next stile and keep ahead up the field. Already wide downland views open before you and close at hand on the left the sloping meadow is terraced into strip lynchets, a relic of medieval farming methods. On the hillside beyond is the chalk figure of George III on horseback. He was a frequent visitor to Weymouth. Cross the next stile and walk up to the signpost at the top of the field. Now the path runs downhill, signed for Osmington Mills, to a gate and

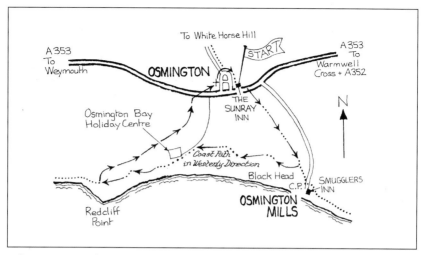

stile. Cross, and continue with the hedge close on the left. When you have crossed the next stile you meet the junction of the two routes of the Dorset Coast Path, indicated by a signpost. Coast Path walkers keep straight on.

The pub walk now follows part of the Coast Path in a westerly direction. Turn right at the post, signed 'Coast Path Weymouth', and follow the path uphill with a hedge on the left. Cross the stile and bear right, following the markers for the Coastal Path. Now you are high on the clifftop above Black Head and, below, landslips have formed a mysterious world of wooded clefts and tiny streams. You look down on the outspread wings of rooks circling their nests in the treetops. The path runs down to pass through the trees. Open boggy stretches are thick with rushes, home for warblers, and more shaded areas are bright with kingcups and irises in season. Boardwalks and bridges lead over stiles before the path climbs to the clifftop once more. Owing to a recent landslip the path now curves further inland round the top of a small inlet. Follow the marker posts in the direction of Weymouth. Then bear slightly left and keep to the marked path as it runs downhill between newly planted trees on your left and the road to the Holiday Centre beyond a hedge on your right. The path descends steps and continues along the edge of the cliff. Look back to see the stone ribs of the Black Head Ledges ruffling the surface of the sea close to the shore. Ahead lies Redcliff Point and, beyond, the town of Weymouth, fringed by its long, sandy beach.

Follow the path as it curves over the open grassy hillside towards Redcliff Point to a stile beside a footpath sign. The sign points straight on for Redcliff Point and Bowleaze Cove and right for Osmington. Do not cross the stile but turn hard right for Osmington. Bear a little left uphill towards a small rise crossed by a clear path. Follow the path over the rise by a marker stone for Osmington. The track leads downhill to pass to the right of Eweleaze Barn. Cross the stile on the right opposite the barn and turn right to walk beside the field with a hedge close on the right (ignore more obvious paths leading uphill on the left). The path leads up to a stile by a footpath sign. Cross the stile and keep ahead with bushes on the right. The Holiday Centre is down the slope on your right. Cross a stile and continue, meeting a crossing fence. Turn left up the field, with the fence on your right, and continue over stiles and along a narrow path to the A353. Turn right along the pavement for about 50 yards then turn left, following the footpath sign, with a fence on the right. When you come to the corner of the fence you will see Osmington church tower across the field. Keep ahead over the field, aiming just to the left of the tower, and cross the stile to walk through the churchyard to the church.

The church, dedicated to St Osmund, has a fine 15th-century tower and many interesting memorials, including one commemorating the Warham family, Lords of the Manor of Osmington in the reign of Henry VII. The ruins of their manor adjoin the churchyard. The outline of windows and fireplaces can be seen and steps lead down to a small wooden door. The ruins have been landscaped into a beautiful private garden.

Leave the churchyard by the lychgate and turn left down Church Street between the rows of charming thatched houses with colourful gardens. Pass Letterbox Cottage (straight from Beatrix Potter!) and turn right along Village Street. Turn right again up Chapel Street to the Sunray, which is on your left.

 THE SUNRAY, OSMINGTON TO OSMINGTON MILLS (1 MILE)

Follow Walk 12 as far as the signpost indicating the junction of the Dorset Coast Path's alternative routes, coastal and inland. (Details of the former, between West Bexington and Osmington Mills, are given at the end of chapter 6.)

Keep straight on here down steps to follow a narrow path between hedges to a road. Turn right to walk down to the coast and the car park for the Smugglers Inn at Osmington Mills, which is in the valley on the left.

WALK 13

OSMINGTON MILLS
The Smugglers Inn
❧

This varied walk begins with a clifftop ramble enjoying magnificent views over Portland and Weymouth Bay and leading to the top of Burning Cliff. The route then turns inland to follow the crest of the downs before descending through woods to return to Osmington Mills.

The name of this tiny hamlet in a steep-sided ravine is misleading! Here are no mills, only a narrow road leading through a fringe of houses to the sea and one of the most charming pubs on the south coast, the Smugglers Inn. The inn has catered for travellers since the 13th century and the old smoke-blackened fireplace, heavy black beams and stout wooden tables and chairs contribute to its old-world atmosphere. In the 18th century the pub was the headquarters of the King of the Smugglers, Pierre Latour, who found the beach close by an ideal landing-place for his contraband.

Today, a warm welcome awaits all the inn's visitors. Families have their own room and restaurant area and outside there is plenty of space for children to play, while the grown-ups enjoy a drink on the patio overlooking the sea. Real ales are Courage Best, Ruddles County, Wadworth 6X and Ringwood Old Thumper. There is a wine list of over 40 wines. The menu is first-class – from vegetarian to à la carte meals. The speciality of the house is sea food, inclu ling locally caught lobster, but examples of many other tempting d shes are Smugglers Beef Wellington, rack of lamb with rosemary a ɪd redcurrant, venison in brandy and blackcurrant sauce and halibɪ t in a cream and orange sauce.

Dogs are welcome on leads in the garder.. Opening times are from 11 am to 11 pm in summer and from 11 am to 2.30 pm and 6.30 pm to 11 pm in winter. The inn offers comfortable ꞉vernight accommodation for which it is advisable to book early. Telephone: 01305 833125.

- **HOW TO GET THERE:** Osmington Mills is on the coast about 2¹/₂ miles east of Weymouth. Approaching from Weymouth along the A353, drive through Osmington village and in about ¹/₄ mile turn right, following the sign for Osmington Mills. Continue for about ³/₄ mile to the inn's car park, which is clearly signed on the right.
- **PARKING:** In the inn's car park.
- **LENGTH OF THE WALK:** 4¹/₂ miles. Two gentle climbs, otherwise easy. Map: OS Landranger 194 Dorchester, Weymouth and surrounding area (inn GR 737818).

THE WALK

Follow the footpath sign 'Coast Path Ringstead, Lulworth Cove' down the steps to the front of the Smugglers Inn. Turn left round the thatched part of the inn, then bear right, following the Coast Path sign. Cross the stile and walk uphill to cross the next stile. Steps lead you to the top of the cliff, giving splendid views of Portland on the horizon. At the foot of the sheer cliff face waves break against the edges of inaccessible beaches. Ahead rises the prominent headland of White Nothe, marking the westernmost point of the Purbeck coast.

A clear path over the turf follows the clifftop and then leads downhill, signed for Ringstead, through low-growing brambles and blackthorn. In the valley you cross a stream flowing through a small wood. Keep straight on over a crosspath to climb the steps ahead. The path becomes a track running past Ringstead village. Paths on the right

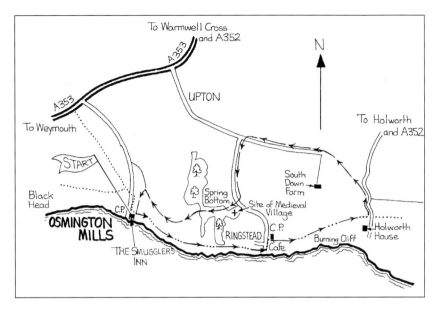

lead down to the beach. Like Osmington Mills, Ringstead was a favourite landing place for smuggled goods, particularly during the Napoleonic wars. Follow the track as it curves left. On the right is a café where you can buy snacks and souvenirs. After about 50 yards turn right as indicated by the marker stone 'White Nothe'. Pass the houses and continue over a field. A pleasant path bears left to wind through copses and over meadows. Keep to the main path to cross a bridge and climb steps to emerge on the grassy clifftop once more. You are now on the top of Burning Cliff. The cliff marks the western end of a huge landslip of vertical boulders and crumbling vegetation covering 115 acres. Burning Cliff derives its name from the years between 1826 and 1830 when it burned almost continuously owing to the oxidisation of oil-bearing shale in its surface.

The path becomes a tarred track leading uphill. When it curves left keep straight on over the grass, signed for White Nothe. The entrance to Holworth House is on the right. Climb the steps to a crossing track.

Leave the Coast Path and turn left here, following the bridleway sign for Holworth. Continue uphill to meet a crosstrack running along the crest of the downs. Turn left for about 50 yards. At this point a lane turns right for Holworth. Ignore this and keep straight on along the downland ridge. Below is a magnificent view of Burning Cliff with Ringstead Bay at its foot. In Thomas Hardy's story *The Distracted*

Preacher Lizzie Newberry sets a gorse bush alight as a signal to warn a lugger carrying contraband that the revenue men were in the vicinity, thus providing an alternative explanation for the name of the cliff!

Continue past the parking area and the turning for South Down Farm, marked 'No cars', to meet a lane still following the ridge. Turn left, following the sign for Ringstead Beach. Continue downhill past a barn on the right. Just before the lane turns left, turn right down a track marked a little way further down 'Private Road'. (It is a footpath.) Just past the 'Private Road' sign bear right to walk through attractive woods. When a path joins on the left our way is straight on, signed for Osmington Mills, but you may like to make a short detour to see the embankments marking the site of Ringstead medieval village, possibly deserted after a French raid. If so, turn left, signed 'Coast Path', and after a few yards the site is in a field on the left, visible over a gate.

Return to the sign for Osmington Mills and follow the pretty woodland path. Ignore another left turn for the Coast Path to keep on over the footbridge in Spring Bottom. Follow the path up the meadow ahead and bear a little left in front of a thatched house to climb a stile. Turn right to follow a path running between houses to meet a lane. Bear right downhill. Just past a caravan site on the left, turn left down a narrow path which runs through the site past wooden chalets. Cross a stile and keep ahead over a meadow towards the corner of a fence. Turn right. The path leads over a stile, down steps, over a footbridge, then up to join the road in Osmington Mills. Turn left to return to the Smugglers Inn with its car park on the right.

 ### OSMINGTON MILLS TO DURDLE DOOR (5¹/₂ MILES)

Follow the route of Walk 13 as far as the turning for Holworth. Keep straight on over a stile, following the edge of the field, then follow the path as it bears a little left uphill, over a stile to the clifftop. A clear path marked 'Lulworth Cove' leads past White Nothe cottages to an obelisk. Take the right-hand path for Lulworth Cove. This drops steeply to Middle Bottom before climbing to the top of Bat's Head. The path drops downhill before climbing up Swyre Head, giving splendid views. A steep descent leads to the foot of a narrow valley called Scratchy Bottom. Take the middle path of the three ahead to climb the cliff and descend past Durdle Door, a natural rock arch.

LULWORTH COVE
The Lulworth Cove Hotel
⋅≈⊱⊰⊱⋅

This is a walk for everyone. It includes visits to three of the most striking features of the Coast Path: Lulworth Cove, Stair Hole, noted for its almost vertical rock strata, and Durdle Door, a limestone archway carved by the sea. The route avoids steep climbs and returns along the clifftop giving magnificent views.

Lulworth Cove must be one of the most visited areas on the Dorset coast, but this horseshoe-shaped bay almost encircled by sheer white cliffs remains beautiful and unspoilt. The Lulworth Cove Hotel stands beside the road leading to the beach. Once a manor house, it dates back 400 years and retains a pleasantly relaxed atmosphere. In earlier days hotel guests would alight at the coach house which until recently stood on the opposite side of the road. The hotel is roomy and comfortable, with blazing log fires in winter. The restaurant is separate from the bar area and there is a garden, screened from the road.

The fish menu includes locally caught lobster and crabs and a tempting home-made fish pie – cod, smoked haddock and prawns in a lemon and parsley sauce topped with puff pastry. Another delicious home-made dish is Cove Turkey Pie, combining turkey, ham and leeks. Snacks, salads and basket meals are also obtainable at the bar. A typical restaurant menu features a choice of starters, such as garlic bread with cheese and prawns, followed by a roast. Sweets may include such delights as black cherry cheesecake. Real ales are from Burton and Tetley. Dry Blackthorn cider is on offer and there is an extensive wine list. Dogs on leads are welcome.

The hotel is open all day in summer, from 11 am to 11 pm, and at other times of the year from 11.30 am to 2.30 pm and 7 pm to 11 pm. Meals are served from 12 noon to 2.30 pm and from 7 pm to 9.30 pm. Overnight accommodation is available. Telephone: 01929 400333.

● **HOW TO GET THERE:** The best approach to Lulworth Cove is off the A352, which runs between Wareham and Dorchester, as this avoids minor roads which cross the Army Ranges. Leave the A352 at Wool to head south along the B3071. Keep straight ahead along the B3070 to pass Lulworth military camp. Drive through West Lulworth village and turn right into the car park at the approach to the cove.

● **PARKING:** In the public car park, opposite the Lulworth Cove Hotel.

● **LENGTH OF THE WALK:** 2½ miles. Map: OS Landranger 194 Dorchester, Weymouth and surrounding area (inn GR 823801).

THE WALK

Turn right from the car park entrance to walk down the narrow street leading to Lulworth Cove, passing the Lulworth Cove Hotel on your left. Continue past the mill pond to the pebble beach. Turn right in front of the fishing boats and lobster pots to walk past the old lifeboat house. Immediately after the lifeboat house, turn right and climb the steps up the cliff. At the top bear a little left over the grass towards a periscope mounted at a lookout point. Pause here to enjoy the magnificent spectacle of Lulworth Cove. Its scallop shape has been formed by the sea eroding a band of soft sands and clays within more resistant limestone and chalk headlands. Beyond the cove is the Isle of Purbeck, a dark ridge of chalk hills. At your feet you look down into Stair Hole, a tide-filled chasm surrounded by contorted rock strata illustrating the famous 'Lulworth Crumple'. These rocks, laid down over 160 million years ago, were folded in this spectacular fashion by the

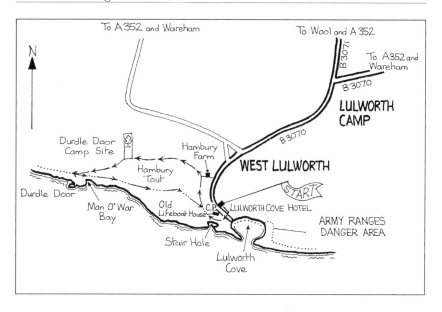

same violent upheavals that formed the Alps.

With Stair Hole on your left, follow the track leading down to a lane. Turn right to walk past the Heritage Centre on your left. Turn left to walk over the car park towards a white path leading uphill. Pass a 'No Camping' notice and continue to a gate and stile at the foot of the hill. Cross the stile but do not follow the path uphill. Instead, turn immediately right, following the sign for 'Durdle Door, avoiding steep and loose section of Coast Path'. Follow the path beside the fence. If it is muddy, better paths run alongside on the hill. Keep to the path over stiles as it curves round the foot of the hill, Hambury Tout. In the valley on your right you will see Hambury Farm. Although the present building is mainly 18th century, there has been a farm here for over 900 years. The wavy roof beam is cut from one giant forest oak. Keep the fence on your right until the path leads up to a signpost in front of Durdle Door campsite and a small wood. Cross the stile and turn left for Durdle Door. The track leads straight ahead through a gate then downhill to the clifftop. The path follows the crest of another scallop-shaped cove, Man o' War Bay, then continues to give a magnificent view of the dramatic rock arch of Durdle Door.

Retrace your steps (Coast Path walkers keep straight on) past Man o' War Bay, following the Coast Path marker stones. When the path divides leave the broad white path taken earlier leading to the campsite and take the right-hand path for Lulworth Cove. The path climbs gradually, giving superb views of Portland and the long sequence of cliffs dazzling white in the sun, ranging from buff to a soft pink in the shadows. These sheer cliffs provide sanctuary for a variety of sea birds including puffins, guillemots, kittiwakes and razorbills. Beside the cliff edge grows wild cabbage, almost confined in Britain to the Dorset coast. The yellow vetch and brilliant blue-flowered Viper's Bugloss provide food for the caterpillars of the tiny Lulworth Skipper butterfly. Keep to the same path as it descends the hillside to return to the car park in Lulworth Cove, opposite the Lulworth Cove Hotel.

 ### DURDLE DOOR TO KIMMERIDGE BAY CAR PARK (7 MILES)

This section of the Coast Path crosses the Army Ranges, closed to the public apart from weekends (except for six), Bank Holidays and the whole of August. Red flags mark the perimeter of the Ranges. When the Range Walks are open there is no red flag at the entrance gates. Keep to the paths, which are clearly defined by posts with yellow rings. Before walking this section of the path it is advisable to telephone 01929 462721 ext 4700 for details.

Follow the route of Walk 14 from Durdle Door to Lulworth Cove. The Coast Path used to continue around the top of the cove but this is no longer usable owing to erosion. The best course is to walk down the road to the beach and turn left to follow the beach to a flight of steps leading up the cliff on the left. You now rejoin the Coast Path. Turn right for the Fossil Forest and Range Walks. After about 50 yards turn right for Pepler Point and the Fossil Forest. The path bears left along the clifftop to one of the entrance gates to the Army Ranges. If the Ranges are open go through and follow the path for Mupe Bay and Kimmeridge. On the beach below are rings of fossilized algae which encircled trees 140 million years ago. The ruins of Bindon Abbey are on the hillside on the left. The path is easy to follow as it curves round Mupe Bay, climbs Bindon Hill, then descends steeply round Arish Mell before climbing to the top of Rings Hill crowned by Flower's Barrow hill fort. A steep descent to Worbarrow Bay is followed by a gentler climb up Gad Cliff with views of Tyneham, occupied by the military in 1943, in the valley on the left. Pass the path to Tyneham and when the path divides at the foot of Tyneham Cap take the lower Coast Path which descends to the low black cliffs fringing Kimmeridge Bay. Continue to the car park.

KIMMERIDGE

The Restaurant at Kimmeridge

❦

This walk along the Purbeck coast, famous for its beauty and its wildlife, will interest all the family. From Kimmeridge village, meadow paths lead to the bay with its fascinating rock pools and intriguing history. Our path then follows the clifftop for 1½ miles before climbing Swyre Head, a magnificent viewpoint. The return route follows the crest of the downs, giving more splendid views.

You will find Kimmeridge tucked away in a wooded hollow at the foot of the windswept Purbeck Hills. The village is small; just a double row of dark-thatched cottages built of local dove-grey stone. As you come down the hill from the car park, past the tiny church with its 12th-century doorway, you may feel there can have been few changes since the village was mentioned in the Domesday Book. But, a delightful surprise awaits you. The Restaurant at Kimmeridge is a real find! This simple thatched cottage, built originally as a school, serves Dorset home-cooking at its finest. Meals are available all day, every day of the week, all the year except Christmas Day. The extensive menu ranges from delicious snacks – try their home-cooked local ham or garlic and tomatoes topped with cheese – to full meals. Specialities include Dorset apple cake served warm with cream, and chocolate and coffee gateau. And their hot chocolate with brandy and cream will work wonders on a cold day! A wide range of special teas includes Lapsang Souchong and Chamomile. The restaurant is licensed with excellent beer on offer. If you wish you can sit outside on a partly shaded terrace overlooking the village street. The Restaurant at Kimmeridge is ideal for families, and dogs can relax happily on the terrace.

Originally the restaurant was called The Seven Taps. It was given this distinctive name by the original owner who, upon moving in, discovered the building did have seven taps. This must have been unusual in such a tiny building! The restaurant car park does get very busy so if you intend to walk use the car park at the approach to the village (see below). Telephone: 01929 480701.

● **HOW TO GET THERE:** Head south from Wareham on the A351 for Corfe Castle. Turn right for Church Knowle and Steeple at the foot of Corfe Castle hill to leave the castle on your left. Drive through Church Knowle and after 2 miles turn left for Kimmeridge. Continue for about a mile. The car park is in a former quarry and is easy to miss as it is unmarked. Pass a joining road on the left and the car park is a few yards further on the left of the road.

● **PARKING:** In the car park at the approach to the village (see above).

● **LENGTH OF THE WALK:** 5 miles. Easy walking but one steep, short climb. Map: OS Landranger 195 Bournemouth, Purbeck and surrounding area (restaurant GR 917798).

THE WALK

From the car park, return to the road and turn right. Opposite a joining road on the right you will see a footpath sign on the left for Kimmeridge. Cross the stile by the sign and walk down the meadow towards the thatched rooftops of Kimmeridge village. The path runs through gates past the little church to the village street. The Restaurant at Kimmeridge (it is also the village stores and post office) is on the left.

Walk down the village street and when the houses end turn right over a stile by a footpath sign for Kimmeridge Bay and the Coast Path.

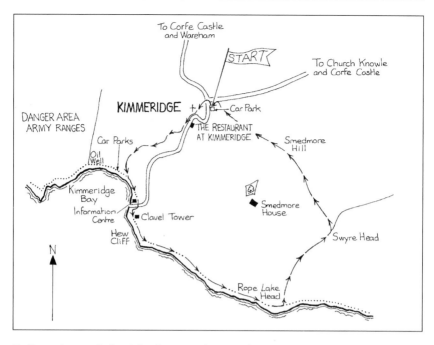

Follow the path beside the meadow with a hedge on the right. Cross the stile and bear left with a hedge close on the left. Continue along the meadow paths, across several stiles, keeping the hedge close on the left and curving downland on the right. Prominent on the coastline ahead is the 'nodding donkey' pump marking the BP oil well, sunk in 1959.

When the path meets a lane turn left for about 60 yards then turn right to cross the car park to join the Coast Path running along the top of the low cliffs overlooking the dark sands of Kimmeridge Bay.

The cliffs of 'Kimmeridge clay' are also dark, composed of alternating bands of shale and yellowish bands of limestone. In the past the presence of shale transformed the peaceful bay into a hive of industry. The Romans mined and polished it to make ornaments and jewellery, and discs from the turners' lathes, known as 'coal money', can still be found. Some shales were used for processing alum and glass-making. During the reign of James I, Kimmeridge supplied the whole of the south of England with drinking glasses. Now the bay is usually busy with divers setting out to explore the rich wildlife on the rocky ledges and offshore wrecks. The shore and rock pools are also worth exploring; colourful with several varieties of seaweed and alive with tiny sea creatures including headlet and snakelocks anemones. Exposed shale surfaces along the shore contain ammonites and other shell fossils.

Bear left along the clifftop to the right of the car park and continue along a narrow path to pass another car park. Take the clifftop path, signed 'Quay and Information Centre'. Steps lead down to a bridge over Gaulter Gap where a stream falls into a small pool. To find out more about Kimmeridge Bay's wildlife visit the Centre. Leave the Centre on your right and walk on to a lane. Cross over and climb the steps, following the Coast Path sign to the top of Hen Cliff. Now you have a fine view over Kimmeridge Bay, backed by the sheer white cliffs of Worbarrow. The path runs close to a stone-built tower reminiscent of a pepper-pot. This is the Clavel Tower built in 1831 by the Reverend John Clavel, then owner of Smedmore House. Later it proved useful as a lookout post.

Follow the clifftop path for 1½ miles to Rope Lake Head. Opposite a Coast Path marker indicating 1½ miles to Kimmeridge, leave the Coast Path and turn left over a stile to take the field path to Swyre Head. The path runs gently uphill at first to a stile by a gate, where you leave the well-defined track. Cross the stile and keep straight ahead uphill with a hedge on the right. The reward for this steep climb is the magnificent view. As you look west, the rugged coastline stretches as far as Weymouth Bay. Inland, Encombe House lies in the heart of one of Dorset's most beautiful valleys, known as 'The Golden Bowl'.

Bear left past the trig point to walk along the crest of the high down, enjoying more wide views inland past Corfe Castle guarding the entrance to the Purbecks to Poole Harbour. In the valley close to the foot of the down is Smedmore House. The track leads down to a road. Turn left for about 50 yards to meet the road to Kimmeridge. Turn left again to the car park.

 ### KIMMERIDGE BAY TO HOUNS-TOUT CLIFF (3¾ MILES)

From Kimmeridge Bay car park follow the route of Walk 15 as far as Rope Lake Head. Keep straight on, following the clifftop path which climbs to give a fine view of the cliffs at St Aldhelm's Head crowned by a row of coastguards' cottages. The path descends to cross the stream at Freshwater Steps at the foot of the Encombe valley. The stream runs down a conduit to cascade over the cliff. The second Earl of Eldon, owner of Encombe House in the 19th century, built the pumphouse close by, now half-buried in weeds but still equipped with its huge wheel, to raise sea water to feed his lakes. A steep climb brings you to the top of Houns-tout Cliff and a stone seat.

KINGSTON
The Scott Arms

This walk through woods and along the crest of a high downland ridge gives splendid views over one of Dorset's loveliest valleys, known as 'The Golden Bowl'. Fine sea views can be enjoyed from the clifftop at Hounstout before the walk returns to Kingston past Chapman's Pool.

Kingston stands proudly on the crest of a ridge of the Purbeck Hills with a magnificent view northwards to Corfe Castle. The cottages, built and roofed with the local dove-grey limestone, overlook colourful hillside gardens surrounded by drystone walls. The village is part of the Encombe Estate. Nearby Encombe House was built by John Pitt, whose father bought the estate in the mid-18th century. In 1807 Encombe passed to the Lord Chancellor, John Scott, who took the title Earl of Eldon.

The Scott Arms dates from the 18th century. It is a large, pleasant pub, attractively draped in Virginia creeper and well known for the breathtaking view of the Purbeck Hills from the garden. Like so many of the best pubs the Scott Arms has a resident ghost, said to be old Granny Bartlett who used to run the village shop.

Real ales include Ringwood Bitter, Greenalls Original and Worthington. Lunchtime snacks and full meals are available with daily specials, such as fresh salmon and venison in red wine. There is plenty of room for dogs on leads in the garden and non-carpeted areas of the pub. Opening times are generally from 11 am to 2.30 pm and from 6 pm to 11 pm during the week, 12 noon to 10.30 pm on Sunday, but these hours are extended during holiday periods. Telephone: 01929 480270.

● **HOW TO GET THERE:** Leave Wareham, heading south on the A351. Drive through Corfe village, then bear right along the B3069 for Kingston. In a little over a mile the B3069 passes the side of the Scott Arms in Kingston village and turns left for Swanage. Leave the B3069 at this point and turn right past the front of the Scott Arms, then turn right again into the car park.

● **PARKING:** In the Scott Arms' car park. If this is full, there is another car park on the left as you approach the entrance to the pub.

● **LENGTH OF THE WALK:** 3½ miles. Easy walking. Map: OS Landranger 195 Bournemouth, Purbeck and surrounding area (inn GR 957796).

THE WALK

With your back to the entrance to the Scott Arms, turn right to walk up the stone-flagged pavement beside the main street of the village. Pass the ornate village pump, following the sign for Encombe. On the left stands the church of St James which appears far too large for such a small village, particularly as you will see another, smaller, church on the skyline on the left! St James' was completed in 1880 as a private chapel for the Eldon family until it was conveyed to the Church Commissioners and consecrated in 1921. The first Earl of Eldon rebuilt the other church in 1833 in the place of a 12th-century chapel. It is now a private house.

Keep straight on past a turning on the right. Just past the drive to Kingston House bear left a little, following the footpath sign 'Hounstout 1¼'. A pleasant, tree-shaded track leads to another footpath sign for 'Hounstout', leading uphill. The track runs along a high ridge through the woods of Kingston Plantation. In early spring the air is heavy with the scent of wild garlic. Hill View nursery, which has a tearoom, is on the left. Already you catch glimpses through the trees of the valley on

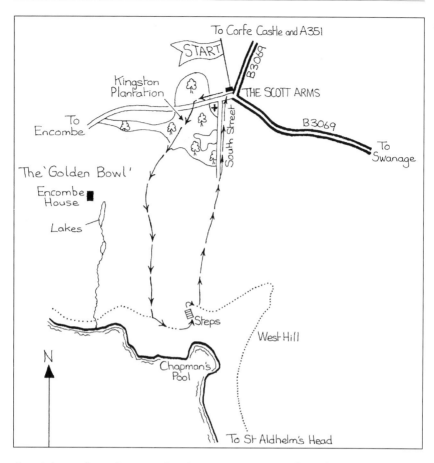

the right and as the woods give way to open downland you have a perfect view over the 'Golden Bowl', the hillsides dropping smooth and sheer to the wooded banks of a stream. At the seaward end of the valley you will see Encombe House, a fine 18th-century building faced in white ashlar and decorated with porticoes and columns. Thomas Hardy knew this country well. Encombe is 'Enkworth House', the home of Lord Mountclere in his novel *The Hand of Ethelberta*. The obelisk on the down was erected by the first Lord Eldon in memory of one of his brothers.

Follow the path over stiles along the crest of the ridge to the clifftop at Houns-tout. There are beautiful views of the coast and a thoughtfully-placed stone seat makes an ideal place from which to admire them. The route now follows the Coast Path.

Continue along the clifftop path as it curves round the edge of Houns-tout. Beyond the jagged rocky outcrops near at hand, a great ridge of cliffs culminating in St Aldhelm's Head juts like a beak into the sea. As you walk, clumps of nettles either side of the path attract swarms of butterflies including Red Admirals, Peacocks and Small Tortoiseshells. Seabirds including Great Black Backed gulls swoop along the cliff face.

The path curves left and descends towards Chapman's Pool, an incredibly blue, scallop-shaped bay, dotted with fishing boats. The surrounding cliffs are dark and sinister and crumble easily, resulting in dangerous landslips. It is said that some coastguards, seeking safety, once asked smugglers not to land their contraband there!

Follow the path down the steps – there is a wooden handrail – to the foot of the hill. Because of landslips, the Coast Path is diverted inland at this point. Turn left over a stile and keep straight on over the meadow, keeping the hill close on your left. Walk up the valley and turn right by the Coast Path marker over a stile. Continue over a causeway to a white lane.

Leave the Coast Path here and turn left. Follow the lane as it runs gently up this strangely remote valley. The only signs of habitation are two cottages perched rather precariously on the hillside on the left. Bear right to cross a stile and continue to a metalled lane. Turn left. Keep ahead, to walk up the valley and through the trees of Kingston Plantation. The road descends into Kingston village, following South Street past St James' church on the left.

When you reach Kingston's main street, turn right opposite the pump to walk down to the Scott Arms.

HOUNS-TOUT TO WEST HILL (1¹/₄ MILES)

From the top of Houns-tout follow Walk 16 to meet the white lane in the valley leading to Kingston. The circular walk turns left here. Turn right along the Coast Path, which bears left, signed for St Aldhelm's Head. The path winds inland up the valley of Hill Bottom, then bears right round Hill Bottom House to a gate. Go through and turn right, signed 'Coast Path and Bridleway'. After the next gate turn left to climb a cleft in West Hill. As you approach the top of the cleft bear right as indicated by a marker stone to the top of West Hill. Turn left to follow the ridge to the point where a path from Worth Matravers joins the Coast Path from the left – about 100 yards.

WORTH MATRAVERS
The Square and Compass

This exhilarating clifftop walk takes you to the most southerly tip of the Purbecks, St Aldhelm's Head, 350 ft above sea level, famous for its views and wildlife. The path rounds the headland to reveal a different scene – massive, cracked and fissured limestone cliffs stretching east to Anvil Point. After a look at the remains of Winspit quarry, the route runs up the Winspit valley to return to Worth Matravers.

Worth Matravers is the most southerly of the Purbeck villages. It stands at the head of a narrow ravine, Winspit Bottom, overlooking a limestone plateau which extends southwards to St Aldhelm's Head. Now a quiet village, it was once at the heart of the thriving Purbeck stone industry. At the foot of the ravine, the cliffs are honeycombed with the tunnels of quarries which were worked until 1950. After a dusty day's work the quarrymen would tramp up the valley to the Square and Compass pub, named after some of the tools of their trade.

Today this gem of a pub is popular with locals and visitors alike. It has been owned by the same family for four generations, and they have carefully preserved its unique atmosphere. Here you find the Dorset of times past. A narrow, stone-flagged entrance way leads to a small serving hatch and two cosy, low-beamed rooms, aglow with enormous log fires in winter and hung with portraits of the many colourful characters who have gathered within their welcoming walls. Among them is a picture of a local legend, Jeremiah Bower, always known as Billy Winspit. From the age of eleven until his death just short of his eightieth birthday he worked as a quarryman and fisherman.

Real ales include Ringwood and Strong Country and in fine weather you can enjoy them on the terrace or in the garden with a view down the valley to the sea. Other drinks on offer include Bulmers Traditional cider. Snacks and a variety of pasties are available. Full meals are served at the Worth Café and Craft Centre opposite the pub, open from 10.30 am to 5 pm all week except Tuesday.

The pub is open from 11 am to 3 pm and from 6 pm to 11 pm and all day on Saturday. Dogs are welcome. Telephone: 01929 439229.

- **HOW TO GET THERE:** Leave Wareham, heading south along the A351. After driving through Corfe Castle village bear right along the B3069 for Kingston. In Kingston keep to the B3069 as it turns left for Swanage. After about a mile turn right for Worth Matravers. In just over a mile the car park is on the right.
- **PARKING:** In the large public car park at the approach to Worth Matravers, a few yards from the Square and Compass.
- **LENGTH OF THE WALK:** 5 miles. Easy walking apart from one steep climb. I include an optional route, not quite so pretty, but avoiding the climb. Map: OS Landranger 195 Bournemouth, Purbeck and surrounding area (inn GR 974776).

THE WALK

From the car park in Worth Matravers turn right down the road to pass the Square and Compass. At the road junction bear right to continue along the main street of the village past the post office. A small duckpond is on your left. On your right a path leads up to the church of St Nicholas. Built mainly around the year 1100, the church possesses a wonderful chancel arch, richly decorated with typical zig-zag carving, and a fine south doorway. In the churchyard you will find a plaque in memory of Billy Winspit and the grave of Benjamin Jesty, the first known person to inoculate his family against smallpox.

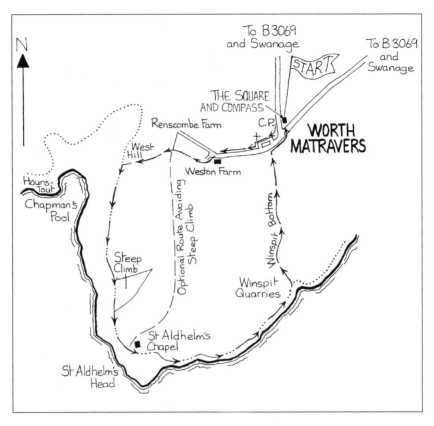

Past the church, the road again bears to the right. Continue along the road (ignore the footpath sign to Winspit) towards a farm. Beyond the fields on the left you will see the hillsides bordering the Winspit valley, deeply scored with strip lynchets. These long, narrow strips were ploughed to grow grain during the land-hungry 12th and 13th centuries. Just past the farm turn left, following the footpath sign for St Aldhelm's Head. After about 50 yards turn right, signed for Chapman's Pool. Keep ahead, following the next sign for Renscombe. The path leads to a crosstrack.

At this point, if you wish to take the optional non-hilly route, turn left along the crosstrack, following the sign to St Aldhelm's Head, and continue for about 1½ miles to rejoin the route of Walk 17 by St Aldhelm's Chapel.

For the main route, cross the track and continue over the field ahead, following the sign for Chapman's Pool. Keep ahead over the next field to meet the Coast Path on the top of West Hill. Turn left to follow the clifftop.

 On your right you have a magnificent view over the tiny, scallop-shaped bay of Chapman's Pool dominated by the smooth crest of Houns-tout. Below Houns-tout, landslips have created a different world of shrubs and trees, known as Molly's Garden.

Continue along the clifftop. The path drops steeply before gaining the top of the cliff once more by a flight of steps. Continue round the clifftop to St Aldhelm's Head and the tiny Norman chapel dedicated to St Aldhelm, 8th-century Bishop of Sherborne, famous for his saintliness and scholarship. Follow the path past the coastguard station. The ruined buildings to the right of the path are the bombed remains of a wartime Telecommunications Research Department where experimental work on radar was carried out. Just after the ruins, the path bears right to continue closer to the cliff edge. Follow the path round the top of Winspit quarry and down steps to the small bay.

After descending the side of the quarry, the path meets a crosstrack. Turn left to leave the Coast Path and walk up the wooded Winspit valley. The attractive woods, dotted with wild apple and cherry trees, surround a lonely cottage, once the home of Billy Winspit. The trees thin as the path climbs higher to run between hillsides of smooth turf. When the path divides, take the right-hand path, signed 'Worth'. A lane leads you past a row of cottages to meet a road in the village. Turn right past a garden on the left and follow the road left past the pond to the main street. Bear right for a few yards, then left, signed 'Kingston', to pass the Square and Compass pub and return to the car park.

WINSPIT TO SEACOMBE ($^3/_4$ MILE)

Follow the route of Walk 17 to the crosstrack beside Winspit quarry. Turn right. The path curves left a little, before turning left again, past a track on the right, to climb steps to the top of the cliff. (The track on the right leads to a former quarry now hosting greater horseshoe bats.) Follow the clifftop path past Seacombe quarry. Cross a stile on the right to skirt a dangerous area of cliffs. The path turns inland for a short distance up the Seacombe valley, then turns right to descend steps.

WALK 18

LANGTON MATRAVERS
The Kings Arms

The fascinating story of the Purbeck stone industry unfolds on this walk. But there is much more to enjoy as the route follows a prehistoric track, descends the beautiful Seacombe valley to the sea and returns along the clifftops past one of the coast's most interesting features, Dancing Ledge.

Stone has been quarried on the Isle of Purbeck for over 2,000 years. The Romans were the first to discover that the topmost layer could be polished to resemble marble and reveal glowing colours of blue-grey, green and red. In medieval times this beautiful stone was used widely in church building and decoration. After the Great Fire of London, the extensive layers of Purbeck limestone were quarried and exported in huge quantities to rebuild the capital. Today, open-cast working quarries can still be seen near Langton Matravers, an attractive village in the heart of the stone country. The 'country warden' of the medieval guild, the 'Ancient Order of Purbeck Marblers and Stonecutters', was chosen from the stone-workers of the parish. The Kings Arms with its thick walls, stone-flagged floors and Purbeck marble fireplace retains the authentic atmosphere of a quarryman's pub. Dating from the early 18th century, it was originally called the Mason's Arms, the first publican was a stonemason. The name was changed during an outburst of patriotic feeling when Napoleon threatened invasion in 1803. Patriotism however had its limits! Many a barrel of smuggled French brandy landed at nearby Dancing Ledge found its way by night to the pub.

The inn offers a choice of four excellent real ales, among them Ringwood beers. Other drinks include a selection of house wines and Blackthorn and Bulmers Traditional cider. Simple, substantial bar meals are served, and various 'specials' such as chicken or vegetable Kiev or gammon and pineapple to be followed by home-made lemon tart or strawberry trifle.

There is a beer garden with an area for children and dogs are welcome. Opening hours are from 11.30 am to 3 pm and 6.30 pm to 11 pm, Sundays from 12 noon to 3 pm and 7 pm to 10.30 pm. En-suite accommodation is available. Telephone: 01929 422979.

● **HOW TO GET THERE:** Langton Matravers is beside the B3069, a mile west of Swanage. Approaching from Swanage along the A351, bear left along the B3069 into Langton Matravers. Alternatively, follow the A351 south from Wareham to Corfe and turn right along the B3069 to drive to Kingston. In Kingston, keep to the B3069 as it turns left to Langton Matravers. The Kings . Arms overlooks the street.

● **PARKING:** In the village near the Kings Arms.

● **LENGTH OF THE WALK:** 3$^1/_2$ miles. Easy walking, with one short climb. Map: OS Landranger 195 Bournemouth, Purbeck and surrounding area (inn GR 999788).

THE WALK

Leave the front of the Kings Arms on your left and walk up the village past the church on your right. The church of St George is full of interest and has beautiful Purbeck marble columns in the chancel. During the 19th century the roof had to be repaired twice as barrels of smuggled brandy stowed above the coved ceiling weakened the joists! Turn left along Durnford Drove, signed for Dancing Ledge. The road is named after Durnford School, one of nine educational establishments which once flourished in the parish. This famous boys' preparatory school did

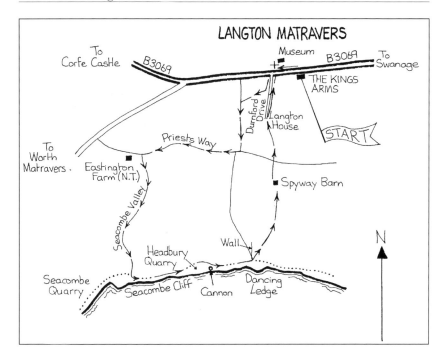

not reopen after the building was requisitioned during the last war.

Pass the last of the houses and turn right over a stile and small footbridge to follow a meadow path with a hedge on the left (ignore narrow paths on the right). When you come to a crosstrack turn left, signed 'Dancing Ledge and the Coast'. Keep to the main grassy path as it runs gently up the field ahead to a gate and stile.

Cross a stile and continue over another stile to a crosstrack. Turn right for Worth. This track crossing Purbeck from Worth Matravers to Swanage dates from prehistoric times. It is known as the Priest's Way as, in the early Middle Ages, Swanage (Swanwic) was a tiny fishing village with a small chapel dependent on St Nicholas' church in Worth Matravers. The priest had to make his way between the two. Keep straight on past a path on the left, signed 'Dancing Ledge'.

Just before you reach Eastington Farm on the left, turn left over a stile by a National Trust sign and footpath marker for Seacombe and the Coast Path. A wide white track leads down the hillside to wind through the lovely Seacombe valley. Keep to this main track as it makes its way past an old quarry-working still ringed by a wall, vital in times past to exclude animals. The track traces the valley floor past joining tracks on the right. A stone Coast Path sign indicates the point where our route meets the Coast Path.

 Ahead is a gate not far from the cliff edge. Do not go through the gate, but turn left to climb the grassy slope of the cliff to cross a stile at the top. Look back for a splendid view of Seacombe quarry, its dark tunnels undermining the cliff face. Here the finer, whiter stone, known as Portland stone, was once quarried to be lowered into boats for transport. Today, the quarry provides nesting sites for seabirds including shags, guillemots, razorbills and kittiwakes.

Follow the clifftop path over the turf cropped short by ponies. The path curves round the top of Headbury quarry through a gap in a wall. If you look down to the flat ledge at the foot of the cliff you will see a cannon mounted on a plinth facing seaward. It dates from Napoleonic times and was found wedged in the rocks by the Dorset author, Rodney Legg. A little further on the path overlooks the wide, flat shelf of Dancing Ledge. This popular picnic spot was formerly a quarry and landing place for smuggled French spirits. The small swimming pool was made for the boys of Durnford School. Follow the Coast Path to a second wall. Here the walk leaves the route of the Coast Path. Before the wall a marker indicates a path on the left to Langton. Do not take this but, following the sign for the Spyway Barn, pass the wall and, bearing a little left, walk diagonally up the hillside to continue up a clear white path to the top. Go through the gate and keep straight on over the fields for the Spyway Barn. A small gate admits you to the farm buildings. Immediately after the gate turn left into a covered area where the National Trust has placed information boards covering the wildlife and history of the area.

Pass the barn and keep straight on for Langton. Cross the Priest's Way and keep ahead along the track, which becomes a metalled lane leading past Langton House, once a school. The lane leads to the foot of Durnford Drove. Retrace your steps up the road to meet the B3069 and turn right for the Kings Arms. Find time to visit the excellent Purbeck Stone Industry Museum behind the church, open on weekdays in April to October from 10 am to 12 noon and 2 pm to 4 pm.

SEACOMBE TO DANCING LEDGE (1 MILE)

Follow the route of Walk 18 from Seacombe to Dancing Ledge. When the circular walk turns left for the Spyway Barn continue straight on for about $1/4$ mile to meet the route of Walk 19.

DURLSTON COUNTRY PARK
Durlston Castle

You are never out of sight of the sea on this walk. The route follows the top of the downs through the park, then continues above the Belle Vue cliffs before descending to Dancing Ledge and returning along the Coast Path past Anvil Point lighthouse and the Tilly Whim caves.

Durlston Country Park, in the south-east corner of the Isle of Purbeck, comprises over 260 acres of open downland and cliffs. Great numbers of sea birds nest on the cliffs, and the 33 species of butterflies include the rare Adonis blue and the Lulworth skipper. Among the wild flowers are several species of orchid. Today the park is owned and managed by Dorset County Council, but originally it was the country estate of a wealthy Swanage stone merchant, George Burt, who bought the land in 1860. He planned a pleasure garden to attract visitors, placing stones inscribed with improving verses at various points and building mock-Gothic Durlston Castle on the headland to provide refreshments. With its turrets, pediments and mullioned windows the castle is worth visiting for its extraordinary architecture alone. And when you add to these a warm welcome and excellent food and ales you have the perfect start to your walk.

Teas, snacks, bar meals and table d'hôte in the restaurant are all available. The fish menu includes mussels and local crab and prawns. Popular dishes include pork fillet in white wine sauce, and lamb and rosemary sausages in a sharp cream sauce. Four real ales are always on offer. A shaded terrace overlooks the sea and there are large gardens. Dogs are welcome on leads. The castle is open from 11 am to 11 pm every day. Telephone: 01929 424693.

- **HOW TO GET THERE:** Durlston Country Park is about a mile south of Swanage town centre. Approaching Swanage on the A351, turn right, following the brown sign to the park. At the roundabout (unsigned) bear left and then follow the signs.
- **PARKING:** In the castle's car park.
- **LENGTH OF THE WALK:** 5½ miles. Easy walking. Map: OS Landranger 195 Bournemouth, Purbeck and surrounding area (castle GR 034773).

THE WALK

Cross the car park to face the entrance gates to the drive leading to Durlston Castle and turn right along the pavement. The Victorian cast-iron bollards beside the pavement are remnants of old London. When George Burt's boats returned to Swanage after carrying loads of Purbeck and Portland stone to the capital they were brought back as ballast. When the road bears right for the information centre (well worth a visit) keep straight on through some of the interesting woodland to be found at Durlston.

Leave the woods to emerge high on the open downland with the sea sparkling many feet below. Go through the gate and keep straight ahead over the grass. On the left, posts mark the east point of a measured mile. Keeping your height, continue to another gate. Go through and walk straight on with a stone wall on your right. Keep ahead to descend towards another gate. Just before the gate, turn left over a small footbridge and follow the main path uphill, bearing right a little to go through a gap in a stone wall. Keep straight ahead now along the crest of the down to go through a gate and leave the Durlston Country Park. The next part of the walk continues over the highest point of the National Trust's Belle Vue cliffs. Just past the gate a marker

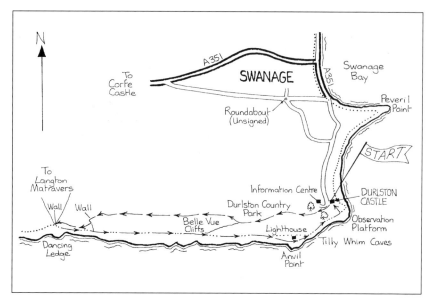

stone indicates 'Upper Path to Dancing Ledge'. An obvious path leads ahead to a gap in a stone wall. Ignore this as it soon leads downhill and we need to keep our height. Instead, bear half-right to walk diagonally up the field to another gap with a marker stone. A track leads ahead, giving splendid views west over Seacombe and Winspit valleys to St Aldhelm's Head. There is a stone wall on your right. The path narrows to trace the top of the hillside before turning inland a little to a stile crossing a wall. Cross the stile and follow the narrow path leading half-left down the hill towards another wall. Just before the wall turn left to walk down the valley to a gap on the right. Go through and almost immediately turn left through another gap to emerge on the short turf of the open hillside. Ignore the grassy track straight ahead and bear half-right to walk diagonally down the hillside to a stile by a marker stone on the edge of the cliff. Cross the stile to walk down to Dancing Ledge, heading west along the Coast Path.

The wide, flat ledge shelving gently into the sea was once part of a large stone quarry. Now it is a delightful place to spend a sunny afternoon sheltered by the quarry caves once a hiding place for contraband.

● Retrace your steps up the Coast Path to the stile and keep ahead along the top of the cliffs. Keep the fence close on your right until it bears left. Cross the stile ahead and follow the cliff path (fence on left) towards the lower of the two western mile marker posts. Pass the post, climb the stile on the left and continue with the fence on the right to go through the gate into Durlston Country Park.

Follow the cliff path to the right of Anvil Point Lighthouse. A stony track leads downhill to former quarry workings before climbing the opposite cliff and continuing past the entrance to the Tilly Whim caves. Now closed owing to rock falls, these are a refuge for rare bats. 'Tilly' was possibly the name of a quarryman and a 'whim' was the crane used by the workers to lower blocks of stone into waiting barges. At the foot of a lane leading up to the Castle is the observation platform. This is a splendid place to observe birdlife and perhaps spot schools of dolphins and Pilot whales.

Leave the Coast Path and turn left towards the castle. Turn right at the crossing path to see George Burt's Great Globe. Poised on the grassy slope of the hillside and surrounded by tablets inscribed by quotations from the scriptures and poets, the globe is 10 ft in diameter and weighs 40 tons. From the globe bear left to the Castle entrance and walk up the drive to return to your car.

 DANCING LEDGE TO BALLARD CLIFF (7³/₄ MILES)

From Dancing Ledge follow the route of Walk 19 as far as the observation platform below Durlston Castle. When the walk turns left keep ahead, following the terraced path along the cliff and passing the Great Globe on the left. Pass the side of Durlston Castle on the left and bear immediately right to walk down a woodland path. Climb steps to a road. Turn right then, after a few yards, right again to cross grassy slopes to the coastwatch tower on Peveril Point. Turn left to follow a road towards Swanage and when the road bears left keep ahead downhill to Swanage sea front. Follow the sea front and bear left up Ulwell Road. Continue past a church as far as a post office. Ignore the footpath to Studland sign and turn right down Ballard Way (not Ballard Road), keeping straight on along a footpath between the houses of Ballard Estate. At a crossroads turn left. Turn right just before number 23 and keep ahead over a field towards the sea. The clifftop path bears left, dips over Whitecliff and begins to climb gently towards Ballard Down. Cliff erosion has resulted in a small diversion. Turn left as a sign indicates over a stile to bear right uphill to a stile on the right. Cross the stile to rejoin the original Coast Path along the grassy slope of the cliff to meet the route of Walk 20 on Ballard Point.

STUDLAND
The Bankes Arms
❦

This is a magnificent walk. The route follows the crest of Ballard Down with panoramic views then takes the Coast Path along the top of sheer-sided chalk cliffs fringed with off-shore pinnacles and arches, including the famous Old Harry stack. Studland Bay, where this walk starts and finishes, is charming and offers an opportunity for safe bathing.

Studland Bay has one of the most attractive beaches on the south coast: a narrow curve of gently shelving sand protected by the chalk stacks off the Foreland, it runs north-east to the tip of South Haven Point at the mouth of Poole Harbour, fringed by low, tree-covered cliffs and dunes. Unlike most coastal villages, Studland does not look seawards but hides itself away down narrow lanes among copse-woodland and thickly hedged fields. But the glory of the village, its splendid Norman church, stands proudly on a rise overlooking the bay.

A friendly, welcoming pub with a genuine village atmosphere, the

Bankes Arms offers excellent food and a choice of six real ales. Locally brewed Poole Bitter is always on tap and when we called other ales included London Pride and Strong Country. Locally caught fresh fish is a speciality. A wide choice of other dishes includes lighter meals such as salads and ploughmans. Dishes for the hearty appetite could be home-made chicken and mushroom pie and whole rainbow trout with prawns and almonds in a brandy and lobster sauce. In summer the pub is open all day from 11 am to 11 pm, in winter from 11 am to 3 pm and 7 pm to 11.30 pm. Dogs are welcome.

This is a pub for all seasons. In summer you can enjoy a drink in the meadow opposite with a glorious view of the bay and in winter you can relax in front of huge log fires. For a longer stay, the pub offers en-suite accommodation. Telephone: 01929 450225.

- **HOW TO GET THERE:** From Wareham head south along the A351 to Corfe Castle. Do not drive up to the village but turn left under the railway bridge along the B3351, signed 'Studland 5 miles'. After you enter the village follow the large signs for the Bankes Arms.
- **PARKING:** In the National Trust car park beside the Bankes Arms (open 9 am to 11 pm).
- **LENGTH OF THE WALK:** 3 miles. Easy walking. Map: OS Landranger 195 Bournemouth, Purbeck and surrounding area (inn GR 038825).

THE WALK

Walk up the lane, leaving the front of the Bankes Arms and the entrance to the car park on your left. Immediately after the car park turn left through the kissing-gate and follow the path beside a field to Studland church. There is a great deal to admire inside this beautiful church with its massive Norman arches and finely groined and vaulted roofs above the chancel and sanctuary. Leave the church by the south porch. Go through the gate and walk down the street ahead past the huge manor barn – once a hiding place for smuggled goods when Studland was in its heyday as a smuggling village – to a road junction. On the left you will see another of Studland's treasures, a modern Celtic-style cross surmounting a Saxon heathstone block. Christian symbols are combined with modern features such as Concorde to express the continuity of the Christian tradition.

Keep ahead, following the lane to the right of Manor Farm, signed 'Swanage'. A narrow lane winds uphill past the houses of the Glebeland Estate to a gate on the left. Turn left through the gate to

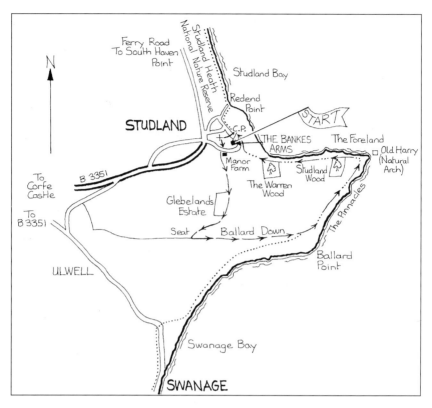

enter National Trust land. Follow the white footpath, bearing a little right up the side of Ballard Down. Turn left to enjoy a splendid ridge walk along the crest of the down. Keep to the same path through a gate to pass a trig point on the right. Go through a gate just after the trig point. Follow the path as it bears a little left and slightly downhill on the open cliffside to meet the Coast Path on the tip of Ballard Down.

● The path descends to give unforgettable views of another aspect of Dorset's varied coastline, the dramatic chalk cliffs of Ballard Point and the Foreland. A clear path leads along the clifftop past the tower-shaped stacks known as the Pinnacles to one of the coast's most famous features, Old Harry, a natural arch of chalk separated from the mainland by a narrow gulf. Beyond Old Harry, like a mirror-image, the Needles front the sea off the coast of the Isle of Wight.

Past Old Harry the path curves left towards Studland. The springy turf is rich in wildflowers which attract hordes of butterflies, including the migrant Painted Lady and Clouded Yellow. Navigation presents no problems as the path continues through copses and between hedges. Glimpses of Studland beach appear on the right and it is difficult to believe that this idyllic spot was once the scene of 'Exercise Smash', a rehearsal for the D-Day landings in Normandy. Studland was 'attacked' with live ammunition and troops and tanks stormed ashore watched by the Allied commanders from a bunker, Fort Henry, on Redend Point not far from the Bankes Arms.

When the path meets the corner of a road in Studland turn right. The road bears left to bring you quickly back to the Bankes Arms and your car.

 ### BALLARD DOWN TO SOUTH HAVEN POINT ($4\frac{1}{2}$ MILES)

Follow the route of Walk 20 as far as the Bankes Arms. Continue past the pub, leaving it on your left, and follow the road past the Manor Hotel. Turn right, following the sign for the Middle Beach, and walk down the lane past the National Trust car park to the beach. Turn left to follow the final section of the Coast Path along Studland's attractive sandy beach. The beach curves a little right before bearing left round Shell Bay to South Haven Point. From here ferries cross the mouth of Poole Harbour to Sandbanks for Bournemouth. Ferries also cross to Brownsea Island.

'Old Harry' rock.

Tourist Information Centres

All local centres can book accommodation for you and will supply up-to-the-minute lists of caravan and camp sites.

Lyme Regis – Guildhall Cottage, DT7 3BS Tel. 01297 442138.

Bridport – 32 South Street, Bridport, DT6 3NQ Tel. 01308 24901.

Weymouth – The Pavilion Theatre, The Esplanade, Weymouth, DT4 8ED Tel. 01305 785747.

Swanage – Shore Road, Swanage, BH19 1LB Tel. 01929 422885.

Wareham – Purbeck Tourism, Town Hall, East Street, BH20 4NN Tel. 01929 552740.

Museums and Heritage Centres

Charmouth Heritage Coast Centre, Lower Sea Lane, Charmouth, DT6 6LL Tel. 01297 560772.

Lulworth Cove Heritage Centre, Lulworth Cove Tel. 01929 400587. There is also an interesting display in a small Centre near the beach.

Kimmeridge Information Centre is housed in a former fisherman's hut on the beach and illustrates the history and wildlife of the area.

Langton Matravers – The Coach House Museum, near the church. This tells the story of the Purbeck Stone Industry and has a reconstructed mine shaft.

Durlston Park Centre – Durlston Country Park, Swanage BH19 2JL Tel. 01929 424443. Fascinating displays and slide shows.

For information on the Chesil Bank and the Fleet, tel. 01305 760579.

For information on the Range Walks and Tyneham, tel. 01929 462721.

Accommodation

Plenty of pub, hotel and bed and breakfast accommodation is available on or near the Dorset Coast Path. As indicated in the book, several of the featured pubs offer accommodation. Given below is a brief list of further availability:

Chideock (for Seatown): Chideock House Hotel, DT6 6HN Tel. 01297 489224.

Eype: Eype's Mouth Hotel, DT6 6AL Tel. 01308 423300.

Burton Bradstock (for Southover): Burton Cliff Hotel, Cliff Road, Burton Bradstock, Bridport DT6 4RB Tel. 01308 897205.

Swyre: The Manor Hotel, West Bexington, Dorchester DT2 9DF Tel. 01308 897616.

Sutton Poyntz: Selwyns, Puddledock Lane, Sutton Poyntz, Weymouth DT3 6LZ Tel 01305 832239.

Osmington: Rosedale, Weymouth DT3 6EW Tel. 01305 832056.

Kimmeridge: Kimmeridge Farmhouse, Kimmeridge, Wareham. Tel. 01929 480990.

Corfe (for Kingston): Mortons House Hotel, Corfe, Wareham. Tel. 01929 480988.

Worth Matravers: French Grass House, Kingston Road, Worth Matravers. Tel. 01929 439443.

YHA

Lulworth Cove – School Lane, West Lulworth, Wareham, BH20 5SA Tel. 01929 400564.

Swanage – Cluny, Cluny Crescent, BH19 2BS Tel. 01929 4221130.

The following three maps indicate the locations of the pub walks.

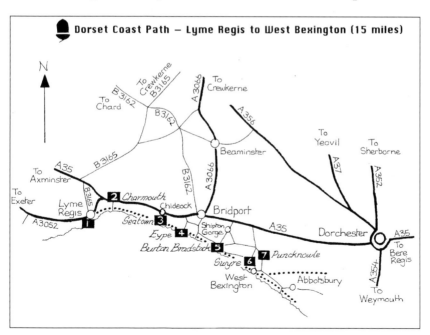

Dorset Coast Path – Lyme Regis to West Bexington (15 miles)

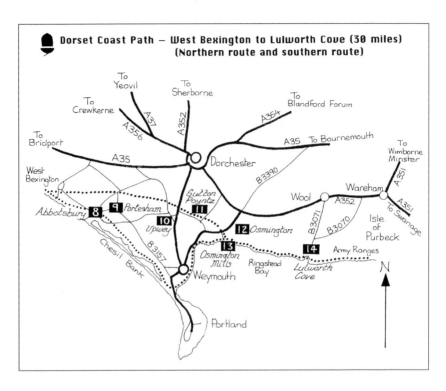

Dorset Coast Path – West Bexington to Lulworth Cove (30 miles)
(Northern route and southern route)

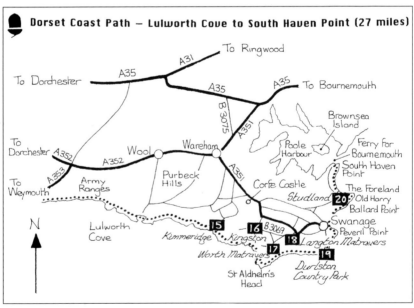

Dorset Coast Path – Lulworth Cove to South Haven Point (27 miles)